His name was

JOHN
FITZGERALD
FRANCIS
KENNEDY

. . . and if he weren't careful, he was going to be expelled from school. His antics had gotten out of hand. The headmaster said: "We have no place here for Public Enemies!"

And John Kennedy's history teacher said: "He was one of those boys who have a certain spark . . . he was one of the rare ones."

Who was this paradox—this young John Kennedy?

He was all boy. But a certain something else set him apart: the something that made him go out for football knowing he'd be trampled by players 60 pounds heavier; that made him a fierce competitor in a swimming meet when he was supposed to be in a hospital bed; that drove him to working night and day on a thesis instead of going to college parties. It was the something that was to lead him to a permanent place in history.

The best introduction to John Kennedy the man is through John Kennedy the boy. You will meet both of them here.

YOUNG
JOHN
KENNEDY

GENE SCHOOR

Illustrated with photographs

MB
A Macfadden-Bartell Book

THIS BOOK IS THE COMPLETE TEXT
OF THE HARDCOVER EDITION

*To my wife Fran
without whose help
this book could not have been written*

●

Acknowledgments

The writer is indebted to numerous friends of
President John F. Kennedy who gave so generously
of their time and effort, provided material, and
furnished recollections of the past. Inevitably some
names may be omitted, but special appreciation is
extended to:

Mr. Kirk LeMoyne Billings and Mr. Ralph Horton,
lifelong friends of the President; Congressman
Torbert Macdonald; Mr. Paul B. Fay, Jr., Under
Secretary of the Navy; Edward F. McLaughlin, Jr.,
former Lt. Governor of Massachusetts; Mr. Thomas
Schriber and Mr. Charles Spalding, friends of the
President; Mr. Earl G. Linebach, Professor and
Mrs. Courtnay Heminway, Reverend Seymour St.
John, Mr. Godfrey Kaufman, and Mr. John R.
Thompson, The Choate School; Mr. Francis Shee-
han, Headmaster of Canterbury School; Professor
Arthur Holcombe, Harvard; Mr. John Cabitor,
Captain, 1937 Harvard Junior Varsity football
team.

●

MACFADDEN BOOKS are published by
Macfadden-Bartell Corporation
205 East 42nd Street, New York, New York, 10017

He wheeled back, his eyes fixed on the ball, leaped high, and pulled it out of the air. Someone in the crowd at the field applauded. This was no ordinary game. These were no ordinary players.

The man with the ball stopped short, reversed his direction, and headed straight for the goal line. Only one opponent blocked a sure touchdown. The opponent was his brother.

"Coming through you!" shouted the ball carrier.

"Waiting for you!" shouted the other.

They raced at each other, the older brother toward his objective, the younger brother to stop him. The ball carrier swerved and twisted sharply to avoid the full force of the power hurled against him, but not enough! Shoulder met shoulder, arm met arm, and both players tumbled to the ground, a mass of flying arms and legs. The crowd did not move. Whatever its fears, they could not be spoken. All the onlookers could do was to watch.

The younger brother was up on his feet first. He offered a helping hand.

"Didn't expect to get past me, did you?" He grinned.

"Next time!" cautioned his brother, brushing the dirt off his pants. "If we get a chance at it!"

"Plenty of guts," said the younger man, "but no brains."

The older brother laughed. They both laughed.

The watching crowd shifted. There were plenty of guts and plenty of brains in both young men—too much to risk in a rough-and-tumble game, and the audience of the historic moment was glad the competition was over.

The skies were clear and brisk over New England. The time was early morning, November 8, 1960. The setting was the family lawn in Hyannisport, Massachusetts, the community playground for the Kennedys, who lived in the row of Cape Cod cottages fronting on Nantucket Sound. The two players were Robert Kennedy, master political campaigner, soon to become Attorney General of his country, and his older brother, President-elect of the United States of America, John Fitzgerald Kennedy.

"Well, now I've seen it all," said one veteran newsman to another in the large crowd that had followed the spectacle. "President-elect four or five hours, and he celebrates it playing touch football with his kid brother!"

"Can't think of a better way," responded the second newspaperman. "Can you?"

"Guess not."

This was the mood that filled everyone there: a gaiety, a curiosity, a sense of wonder, and a quality of expectancy that most resembled the election of Franklin Delano Roosevelt some twenty-eight years before. Here was a young man, forty-three years old, the youngest man ever elected to the nation's highest office. This was reason enough to draw the huge throng of reporters, broadcasters, TV cameramen, political campaigners, curiosity seekers, and just plain folk and friends. But Jack Kennedy was out there playing ball—touch football—like any ordinary American citizen on a Saturday afternoon or a Sunday after church.

"The President made a nice catch," said one old Hyannisport neighbor to another.

"He should have gotten away from Bobby," said the other.

"It's a wonder they can move, never mind walk or run or jump, the way they've campaigned these past ten months."

The political campaign Robert and John had been through was perhaps the most strenuous one in the whole history of American politics. Both men were tired. Lines drawn by months of sleepless nights showed on their faces. Weariness was in their bones. But their hearts were young, and the tensions, the doubts, the hopes that came with Election Day and grew with the long night of counting and tabulating returns had been resolved in the early-morning hours. Exhilaration, joy, love, consideration, and tenderness were the passwords in the Kennedy quarters this memorable November morning.

Jacqueline Kennedy, the beautiful wife of the President-elect and soon to become a favorite with the people and with government officials of many countries, had gone to bed before the others in the early-morning hours.

Caroline, their first-born, was three. There was another child on the way, however, and Jacqueline put up only token resistance to retiring before the final election returns were in.

She was at the door, however, with Caroline to greet the football players as they came off the field.

"Good morning, Mr. President."

Jack smiled and avoided the reference to his election.

6

"It's easy to misplace a wife and child around here," he said, laughing at the happy crowd milling about.

The President-elect looked around at the newspapermen, TV men, neighbors, tourists.

"Do you think we can get away from them now?" he asked.

They might have been able to at another time, only not this morning after election; but Caroline, the three-year-old with a mind of her own, seized her father's hand.

"Let's take a walk along the beach," she demanded.

"All right," said her father, "but it will have to be a short walk today. I've a lot of things to do, and there are a lot of people waiting for me."

Caroline made no reply. She had her father. It was a simple matter to lead him where she wanted to go. Things and people could wait. Caroline and the President-elect, hand in hand, newsmen and photographers following close behind, began one of the least private walks—in the history of father and daughter promenades—along the beach.

"I want a piggyback ride, Daddy," said Caroline.

He may have been President-elect to the whole world; he was simply "daddy" to Caroline.

"Sure," said the man just elected to the most responsible post in American government. "Up you go!"

And up went Caroline on her daddy's back; and behind him the cameras went, "Click! Click! Click!"

There wasn't a father or mother in the whole of the United States who didn't warm to the picture or to the story of it. John Fitzgerald Kennedy was steel and iron, as well as heart, campaigning against an opponent, battling his adversary in whatever town, city, county, or state he visited. He thought fast, talked fast, always with the facts at his command, always to the point, always toward the victory he sought. With Caroline, he was like any other father, something to be shaped and molded to his little daughter's least wish.

Down to the beach, along the sands, and back again they went, and then, at last, into the house for the few quiet minutes he could take before the long, hard schedule of statements, conferences, pictures, and more statements, more conferences, more pictures. Jack Kennedy would not, in fact, become President of the United States for some ten weeks. January 20, 1961, was the date of the inauguration, the ceremony that would swear him into the presidency and the White House, but the responsibilities that are part of the

7

most important office in the entire world had already begun to fall on the shoulders of this young American.

It was nearly three o'clock in the afternoon when the members of the President-elect's family motored to the local National Guard Armory. The TV camera recorded it all and sent out the picture to every home in the United States. John Fitzgerald Kennedy stepped up to the battery of microphones. For the first time, the entire nation witnessed the cost of the campaign in the weariness the President-elect could not conceal, did not try to conceal. He spoke briefly.

He replied to the congratulatory telegram of Richard Nixon, Vice-President of the United States and the defeated candidate for the presidency, saying: "I know that the nation can continue to count on your unswerving loyalty."

He read President Dwight D. Eisenhower's wire of congratulations, and to "Ike" he said, "The whole country is hopeful that your long experience in the service of your country can be drawn upon further in the years to come."

He thanked all the people who had worked for his election, and then, addressing himself to all the people, he said, "To all Americans I say that the next four years are going to be difficult and challenging years for us all. The election may have been a close one, but I think that there is general agreement by all our citizens that a supreme national effort will be needed in the years ahead to move this country safely through the nineteen-sixties."

His words, as always, were to the point and well chosen. His face looked determined, almost grim, as he promised, ". . . every degree of mind and spirit that I possess will be devoted to the long-range interests of the United States and to the cause of freedom around the world."

This was his first message as President-elect to his people. Now he could relax, or try to.

A tired smile broke across his face.

"So now," he said, "my wife and I prepare for a new Administration, and for a new baby."

A burst of applause shook the old armory as the young President-elect led his wife off the dais and, still followed by the crowd of reporters and TV men, friends and neighbors, drove back to their cottage for a few hours of much-needed rest.

"How do you feel now?" asked one of the newspapermen who just wouldn't go home.

"I'll answer that," said Eunice, the President-elect's sister, mercifully shutting the door for her weary brother.

"I'm just beginning to catch my breath. We're all just beginning to catch our breath."

The Kennedys, ever since Patrick Kennedy, the first of them to land on these American shores, have maintained a fast pace. Their story is one of constant battle and victory. But no battle had been harder fought, no victory so glorious, as the battle and the victory that had made John Fitzgerald Kennedy President of the United States.

Among themselves, the Kennedys' elation over this tremendous achievement was a quiet one, touched with the humility of a profoundly religious family. Joseph P. Kennedy, ex-Ambassador to the Court of St. James's in London and father of the President, wept unashamedly. With the birth of his first son, his dream for the boy had been the presidency of these great United States. John Fitzgerald Kennedy's victory was the realization of that dream.

★ ★
2
★ ★

In the board room of the Bethlehem Steel Company's Fore River Shipyard at Quincy, Massachusetts, young Joseph Patrick Kennedy listened intently to the speaker and nodded his head in agreement. Just twenty-nine years old, surrounded by men much older, more seasoned in the business, he weighed the words he heard and approved of them.

The year was 1917. America was joined with England and France in the first of the two great wars against Germany and her Central Powers. The man at the head of the table had come to inspect the Fore River Shipyard, of which Joe Kennedy was assistant manager, and to address those responsible for hastening and intensifying the war effort.

He spoke to the point.

"The English, the French, our other allies, have been heroic in their struggle against the invading German armies," said the speaker. "For two and a half years they have held back the marauding Hun. They look desperately now toward us and our great country for assistance. That assistance, before we can muster our own army, must come in the form of ships, ships we build, ships we load with food and arms, ships we load with men!"

The speaker was young Franklin Delano Roosevelt, Assistant Secretary of the Navy. He was tall, handsome, healthy, and his speech was direct and vigorous.

"We have been involved in this war, this war for democracy, for a long time. True, it is only since April of this year that our government declared war on Gemany, but the whole history of our country has been a struggle for democracy."

Roosevelt could move an audience if with nothing more than his personality, his forcefulness, his passion for the goals he set himself. He was the kind of man who knows what he wants and goes after it; he was a Joe Kennedy man.

"You've been doing a fine job at this shipyard. I want you, the United States expects you, to do an even better job! I know you can and you will do it!"

They applauded the speaker. They made promises they would keep. They shook his hand.

For the assistant manager of the Bethlehem Steel plant, it was no mere formality to shake the hand of the young Assistant Secretary of the Navy; it was the beginning of a long and fruitful friendship.

Joe Kennedy's grandfather had come from New Ross in Ireland, with little more than the clothes he carried on his back, for the freedoms the still-young land of America promised the brave young men and women who came to her shores. Joe's father, Pat Kennedy, inherited his father's courage and initiative. Orphaned, with three sisters to support, quickly and surely he moved to the front as a leader of the growing population of the Boston Irish. Six times he was elected to the Massachusetts State Legislature. He was appointed fire commissioner, street commissioner, election commissioner. He became the man behind the man in office.

When Joe Kennedy was just five years old, he woke one night, roused from sleep by the noise and shouting in the living room.

It was his father, Pat Kennedy, and Honey Fitzgerald, the two big names in Boston politics, in one of their frequent political battles. Little Joe stood in the door, listening to them for fully five minutes before they noticed him.

"What are you doing up so late?" said Pat Kennedy. "Off to bed with you! You're too young to get into politics."

He picked up the youngster and deposited him back in bed.

"He isn't going to hurt you, is he?" asked the boy.

Pat laughed.

"We're just having a friendly talk," he said. "Nothing for you to worry about. Now you get some sleep."

Little boys have a way of remembering things for a long time. It may have been that "political talk" between Pat Kennedy and Honey Fitzgerald that started young Joe Kennedy on the road to high office.

The Kennedy house was always jammed with politicians, aldermen, commissioners, congressmen, assemblymen, senators. The talk wasn't always quite so loud, and young Joe became the pet of all the visitors to the house.

"What are you going to be when you grow up, young fellow?" they asked him. "Become mayor or governor?"

"I'm going to play first base for the Boston Red Sox," he answered, and the visitors patted his head and laughed.

But young Joe was serious about baseball. He was also

11

quite serious and successful in the art of making the money he felt he needed. At the age of nine, he hawked refreshments on a Boston excursion boat. At fifteen, he engineered a plan to provide new uniforms for the Assumptions, the sandlot baseball team he captained, selling 3,000 tickets at 25¢ apiece to a "championship" sandlot game in the Locust Street Park.

Success on the diamond and success in business kept Joe loyal to his ambition. Twice elected captain of the Boston Latin School's baseball team, he won the all-Boston high school batting championship with a lusty batting average of .570. It was Mayor Honey Fitzgerald, the man who had argued with his father, the man who was to play an even more important role in the life of Joe Kennedy, who presented the trophy to the young lad.

It was at Harvard, where Joe roomed with the great football star, Bobby Fisher, that his ambition soared when he was elected captain of the Crimson nine. It was here, too, that that ambition came to an abrupt end.

The Harvard baseball team was playing a practice session against the mighty American League Boston Red Sox.

Joe sat on the bench, worried.

"Is something wrong with my eyes?" he asked a teammate.

"I don't see anything."

"I can't see that ball he's pitching," complained Joe.

"Who can?"

Smokey Joe Wood, one of the really all-time greats of baseball, was pitching for Boston. He was just about the fastest pitcher in the game.

"He doesn't look so fast from the stands," commented Joe, watching the great star wind up and bullet the ball past the batter. "He doesn't just throw the ball; he smokes it across the plate!"

Still, for all his disappointment in the way he played against the Red Sox, Joe Kennedy didn't quite give up his dream of playing professional baseball until his arm went lame.

"I don't know how, but it happened," he said. "You can't play first base with a lame arm, or anywhere else in the field. I had to forget about playing in the big time, but I love the game. I suppose I always will."

After a while, he added, "There's little place in the world for someone who comes in second best. The winner gets all the glory."

Joe Kennedy went after that glory. With baseball as a career finished, he turned to finance.

"I'll make my first million by the time I'm thirty-five," he announced solemnly to his roommate, Bobby Fisher, as he wrote the numbers large in the notebook he had reserved for his course in business and banking.

"I'll bet you will!" said Bobby Fisher, who needed no convincing.

Joe and another classmate, Joe Donovan, had run sight-seeing buses to Lexington and Concord during summer vacations from school. They had earned, between them, $5,000, carrying tourists to the two most famous battlegrounds of the American War for Independence. Five thousand dollars is a great deal of money today. When Joe Kennedy was a student in Cambridge, it was a small fortune. It wasn't until Joe got out of Harvard, however, that he really began the career that would make him one of the richest men in America.

His first job earned him $125 a month as a state bank examiner. He earned and he learned. He borrowed $45,000 from friends and relatives, who had faith in him and in his ability, and bought stock in the Columbia Trust Company. At the age of twenty-five, he became the youngest bank president in the history of banking.

He met Charles Schwab, president of Bethlehem Steel, and Mr. Schwab made him assistant manager of the big Fore River Shipyard. He met Galen Stone of Wall Street, and Mr. Stone put him in charge of his Boston brokerage office. Both men were taken with the charm, the intelligence, the forcefulness of the young man. Joe Kennedy moved forward with them. He was on his way to his first million, and many more.

It was while he was still at the bank that he married Rose Fitzgerald, the daughter of John F. Fitzgerald, better known as "Honey Fitz" or just "Fitz," the first native born Irish-American elected to the mayoralty of Boston. The courtship and the marriage, however, were not accomplished without some pain and difficulty.

The Kennedys and the Fitzgeralds were the best of oldtime friends, and sometimes enemies, in and out of the club-rooms of political Boston. Each man was a power, and powers will clash. The picture of Rose Fitzgerald, adorning Joe Kennedy's desk, was the barometer of the Pat Kennedy-Honey Fitzgerald relationship.

One day Joe Donovan walked into Joe's room. He picked up Rose's picture.

"Don't touch it!" yelled Joe.

"You've got her face to the wall!"

"I've been forbidden to see her," said Joe Kennedy.

"They've been arguing again!" Donovan laughed.

"It's no laughing matter!" objected Kennedy.

They were the Romeo and Juliet of Boston; their families, the Montagues and Capulets of New England.

Rose Fitzgerald and Joe Kennedy, the young man beginning to climb the ladder of success, weathered the storms, the feuds, the political wars. In a magnificent moment of truce between the two great warriors of Boston politics, the two young people were married. The year was 1914, William Cardinal O'Connell officiated at the ceremony. Joe borrowed $2,000 to set up his own home in the more modest section of Brookline, and the Fitzgeralds and the Kennedys were joined in their destiny.

Rose Fitzgerald Kennedy was an accomplished young woman. She had studied music in Aix-la-Chapelle, had been graduated from the Sacred Heart Academy in Manhattanville, spoke French and German fluently. She knew, too, how to make a home and raise a family that was to grow to nine beautiful children.

Her first child came a year after her marriage. It was a boy. He was named after his father, Joseph Patrick Kennedy, Jr.

"He'll be the first Kennedy to become president of the United States," said the proud father, whose ambitions never reached for anything but the very top.

"Don't rush him," said the young mother, fondling the handsome infant.

"You never know," insisted Joe. "We're all winners in this family. "

The second son came a short two years after the birth of Joe Jr. They named him John Fitzgerald Francis, and John Fitzgerald Francis Kennedy, born May 29, 1917, was destined to fulfill the dreams of his father and of "Honey Fitz," of all the American-Irish who first sought a place for themselves in the political sun.

"There's little place in the world for someone who comes in second best," repeated Joe Kennedy. "The winner gets all the glory."

All their children would grow up to be winners, John Fitzgerald Kennedy the biggest winner of them all.

3

"He's here!" yelled little six-year-old Jack Kennedy, racing for the front door.

He had been standing at the window all morning, waiting for the arrival of Grandpa Honey Fitz.

Big brother Joe, all of eight years old, dropped the book he was reading.

"Last one to Grandpa is a dummy!" he challenged, grappling for the doorknob already in his brother's hand.

"I saw him first!" protested Jack, but protest wasn't going to do him any good, as the two young brothers shoved and pushed and elbowed to be first to greet the "Little General" as all Boston called their grandfather.

Father Joe Kennedy watched. He said nothing. They would battle it out. They had been battling it out ever since they were both able to walk. Joe would win. He always won. He was two years older. But Joe Sr. had seen Young Joe put up his fists for his younger brother more than once; and he would do it again. It was the normal thing for two brothers, just two years apart, to be in constant competition; but the blood was thick between them, and beneath all the fuming and scrapping, they were as close to each other and as loyal to each other as any two brothers could be.

Joe Jr. had the knob at last.

"Now try to catch me!" he shouted triumphantly, and raced out to meet Grandpa.

"Wait till I'm bigger!" roared back Jack, close on his heels. "Just you wait!"

Grandpa was already on the walk, and the boys were no more than a step apart.

"I'm first!" yelled Joe.

"I'm first!" yelled Jack, undaunted.

"And you're both first with your old grandpa!" declared Honey Fitz. "And you're a fine pair of lads, with all that hurrying in your fine legs. Speed! That's what counts. Speed to where you're going. Time waits for no man."

It was a long speech for two impatient youngsters, and there was more to come, but the boys were used to Grandpa

Fitz's speeches. He liked to talk and they liked to listen, especially since the listening was always rewarded with a great time one place or another in or about Boston.

The small man threw his arms around the boys.

"What a sight you are for these old eyes of mine! Two strapping young men! Sure and you'll be playing baseball for the Red Sox before I've had time to turn my back on you!"

His daughter Rose had been his great pride and joy. Now her two sons were the apple of his eye.

"Sing us a song," said little Jack.

They knew the way to Grandpa's heart.

"Is it a song you want?"

This was a mere formality. He gathered the rest of his grandchildren around him, Rosemary who was only four, Kathleen, three, and Eunice who was two.

"And what song would you have me sing?"

This, too, was a question that needed no answer.

" 'Sweet Adeline!' " chorused the boys and Rosemary and Kick, as Kathleen was nicknamed.

" 'Sweet Adeline' it is then," said Grandpa, and there he was, for all the world as though on a vaudeville stage, singing his favorite song. "Sweet Adeline . . ."

Honey Fitz was not a great singer, but his voice was good, and "Sweet Adeline" was the song his daughter Rose had taught him. He sang it on street corners when there was an election rally; he sang it in club rooms, in private homes, or at conventions, at the gayest and at the soberest meetings. "Sweet Adeline" was Honey Fitzgerald's trademark, and if he didn't sing it at once, the band would strike up the music and there would be Honey delivering the song once more to the consternation of his antagonists and to the delight of his friends, who were many and legend.

"How about going to see the ball game?" asked Grandpa, after his song was properly applauded. This was the treat for the day.

"Great!" shouted Joe Jr.

"Great!" echoed kid brother Jack. "When? Where?"

"Today, you dummy!" yelled Joe. Then he quieted down. Grandpa Fitz, a ready man for any battle in the political arena, didn't like to see his grandsons fight.

"The Red Sox against the Philadelphia Athletics," said young Joe. He was displaying his superior knowledge. "It's the opening game of the season."

"Let's go!" And out they went, each holding one of Grandpa's hands, each as proud as he could be.

The ball park, for Grandpa, was just another part of his great bailiwick.

"How are you, Fitz?"

"Hello, Honey!"

"Great to see you, General!"

Everyone in the ball park knew Grandpa. But everybody, everywhere they went, knew Grandpa. The boys' hearts beat faster with excitement as they proceeded to their seats in the ball park.

"Can I get my scorecard autographed, Grandpa?" asked Joe.

"Mine, too?" asked Jack.

"I think it can be arranged," said Grandpa, waving his hand to his great audience, fans and players alike. "We've got to stand up now. The National Anthem."

The Stars and Stripes rose high in centerfield. The huge crowd in the stands, the players on the field, bared their heads and stood at attention. A mighty voice sang "The Star-Spangled Banner." There was a roar of approval and then what seemed to the boys like a veritable mob of people advanced on their box.

"That's Frank Chance!" said young Joe Kennedy excitedly. "And Lefty O'Doul!"

"And Bullet Joe Bush and Mr. Cornelius McGillicuddy," added Grandpa Fitz.

"Connie Mack?" asked little Jack, still unsure of the meaning of the moment.

"Of course, you silly!" exploded his impatient big brother. "And Sad Sam Jones and home-run slugging Tilly Walker!"

They were all coming over. Manager Frank Chance, of the great Tinkers-to-Evers-to-Chance double-play combination, Connie Mack who made baseball history, Joe Hauser, Jimmy Dykes, Everett Scott, slugging George Burns—the baseball heroes of every youngster in America—they were all coming over to shake the hand of Boston's great Honey Fitz.

"These are my two strapping grandsons," he said, introducing the boys to Bing Miller, Howard Ehmke, Ed Rommel, and all the other greats of the diamond who crowded around them. "I think they'd like your autographs."

"Sure thing. Glad to meet you."

"Nice to know you!"

"Good to say hello to Honey Fitz's boys!"

They shook the boys' hands and wrote their names on the scorecards they were offered.

"You want to watch them," said Honey. "They'll be trying out for your positions on the team before you know it!"

The boys blinked to the flash of cameras.

Frank Chance gave the ball to Honey Fitz. Honey threw it out across the diamond. There was a loud cheer, the band struck up "Sweet Adeline," and the baseball season had begun officially in Boston.

"Will our pictures be in the papers?" asked Jack.

"Grandpa's picture!" snapped Joe.

"Maybe yours, too," said Grandpa.

They were tired little boys when they got home from the game, but little boys recuperate quickly, and they were at their grandpa for more.

"Make a speech! Make a speech, Grandpa!"

"Fellow citizens!" Honey Fitz could make a speech at the drop of a hat. "Fellow citizens!"

The young Kennedys applauded. That was the way it was done at all the rallies they attended with Grandpa.

"If I am elected," said Fitz.

"Hurray for Grandpa!" His audience was enthusiastic.

"You'll have a friend at the state capital."

"Everybody votes for Grandpa!" yelled the joyous family, Rosemary, Kathleen, and even little Eunice joining the electorate.

"Sure and you want a friend at the state capital," insisted Honey Fitz.

"Hurray! Hurray!"

Joseph Kennedy, Sr., kept himself in the background of the political arena, but his sons and daughters moved early into the life of Massachusetts politics, its campaigning, its backroom battles, its elections. They saw none of the inner party struggles Joe Sr. had witnessed as a boy, but the deepening sense of the meaning of America, its history and its purpose, came to them at home through their mother and father, who spared nothing in their efforts to give their children the best possible education, a concern with the affairs of their country, and a love for its traditions and its freedoms.

"We're going to Bunker Hill this afternoon," Rose Kennedy would say, gathering her children for a trip to one of the shrines of American history.

"This is the very spot of the Boston Tea Party," she would explain, as the children looked into the water for some possible souvenir of that glorious raid against tyranny.

"Here is where the Pilgrims landed."

"This is the famous steeple."

" 'One if by land, two if by sea,' " said Joe Jr., indicating he knew his lesson.

"That was Paul Revere's ride," said Jack, not to be out-done.

"Show us the place where the children threw rocks at the British soldiers, Mother!" cried Rosemary.

The Kennedy children knew every historic landmark in Massachusetts, and they could detail every important event by heart. They knew, too, as well as children can know, the current problems besetting their own country, which had only recently become the world's leading power, and world problems also.

"Why didn't we join the League of Nations, Dad?" asked Joe one day when he was a little older.

"Would you have voted for it, Joe? Why?" countered his father.

"How about Daniel Boone?" cut in Jack.

He didn't want to be left out of the talk.

"How *about* Daniel Boone?" asked his patient father. "How much do you think he helped this country to grow west-ward?"

The girls would join the conversations as they grew older. Dinnertime was as good a time as any to learn one's coun-try's history.

"Grandpa Kennedy," said Joe Sr. to his eagerly listening family, "never had the chance to go to school for very long, but he knew what it meant to be well schooled, to learn. Sometime you must ask him to show you some of the books he has read on his own. He was always reading—he used to read history books especially. And he never complained about the lack of time to read. He made that time. Do you think he could have gotten where he is without all that read-ing?"

It was a rhetorical question. The Kennedy children did not need to answer. They came from a family that understood the need, the value, the pleasure of learning; they moved in the same tradition through their schooling, the dinner-table dis-cussions, and reading *The New York Times. The New York Times* was Rose Kennedy's special contribution to the educa-tion of her children.

" 'All the news that's fit to print,' " she read. "And that's history, too."

The New York Times had it place in the day's schedule, along with her schedule of the children's appointments with their doctors and dentists.

"You'll find the past in your history books," she said, open-ing the pages of the daily paper for all her children to look on. "The present is in your newspaper. We'll all help, I hope, to make the future."

And, in the tradition of all families, the oldest son assumed responsibilities for the education of the younger children, especially when his father was away on business, and Joe Sr. was away often in his busy career. This responsibility had its advantages for both mother and son, but its disadvantages as well.

"When Dad's not here, I'm the boss!" Joe Jr. announced. He took his task and his authority seriously.

It was all right with Rosemary, Kick, Eunice, Pat, Bobby, and Jean in their time; Jack was a bit harder to handle.

"Why can't I sail the boat?" he demanded, holding his balance against the wash of the water.

"You'll sail it when you know how!" yelled Joe Jr. He had a bit of temper. He was easily riled.

"And you're going to tell me when!" challenged Jack.

"I'm telling you right now to get out of that boat!"

"You and who else?"

"Dad's not here," warned Joe. "I'm boss!"

"Not for me, you aren't!" snapped Jack.

Quick as a hare, Joe was at his side. A sweep of his hand and Jack was in the water.

Jack shook the water out of his hair and swam around to the starboard.

"Give me your hand!" yelled Joe.

"Got you mad, didn't I?" Jack smiled.

"Pipe down!" ordered Joe.

But the scowl left his face quickly. He was easily roused to anger, but he was as fast to come out of it.

"Let me show you how to sail this boat, and maybe you can learn."

Being a big brother to Jack wasn't easy. Joe was earnest and worried about his duties. Jack was his constant challenger, sometimes out of a sense of rebellion against this temporary authority, sometimes out of sheer mischief, and it wasn't always Joe who got the best of it.

One evening, the dessert was served while they ate the main course. The dessert was chocolate pie, covered with whipped cream. Joe Jr. had his father's passion for chocolate, especially chocolate pie with whipped cream. He enjoyed even the anticipation of eating it. There it sat while he finished his meat and potatoes. Jack sat next to him. Jack had a fondness for chocolate pie, too. He ate his meat and potatoes and eyed both pieces of pie, Joe's and his.

Joe ate slowly, enjoying fully the promise of the dessert. Jack had to be told he was eating too fast. He slowed down, but still he finished his main course and his pie while Joe dallied with his.

"Excuse me," said Jack, rising, as if to leave the table.

Then, swoosh! He reached for Joe's pie, scooped it up, and stuffed it, whipped cream and all, into his mouth.

"Hey!"

Joe was too startled to move, and Jack dashed out of the room, swallowing as he ran.

"I'll get him!"

Joe was after him in a flash.

"I'll get you!"

Across the lawn raced Jack, Joe closing in on him; up to the water's edge, along the breakwater running some twenty-five yards into Nantucket Sound.

The whole family was at the water's edge by this time, Rose and the girls, Rosemary, Eunice, Kathleen.

"Watch out, Jack!" yelled Kick.

"Careful, Joe!" shouted Rosemary.

With Joe's temper and Jack's contrariness, anything might happen; and the tide and the water of Nantucket Sound were rough and treacherous at the end of the breakwater.

"Come back, Joe!" commanded Rose Kennedy.

"Come back, Jack!" pleaded Eunice.

But Jack was at the very end of the stone wall by now, and Joe advanced on him with fixed intent and purpose.

"Joe!"

"Jack!"

They weren't more than a few feet apart.

Jack looked into the water; it was dangerous and dark out there, but it was the only escape.

Joe looked at Jack, the whipped cream smeared all over his face.

"Why did you have to do that?" yelled Joe. "Why did you have to steal my pie?"

And then he laughed.

He didn't know which was more ridiculous, his anger or his brother's fearless but whipped-cream-covered face.

"Better come in and get your mouth washed," he said, and turned on his heels and walked back home.

Joe had an Irishman's temper. He also had an Irishman's sense of humor. For all the scrapping, for all the fighting, he was a real big brother. Jack admired him and loved him and, with the rest of the family, recognized the possibility of greatness in the Kennedy first-born.

"He has the making of a great political leader," Joe Sr. said. "He could become President of these United States."

The ambition for the presidency in the Kennedy household was born with Joe Jr. History cut Joe Jr.'s career short; his kid brother, his closest rival, his closest friend, took up that ambition and fulfilled it, but there were many years, many changes, many ups, many downs, before that eventful day.

4

"Merrily we roll along, roll along, roll along . . ."

Everybody was rolling. Joseph Kennedy was leaving Brookline and Boston. The brilliant young man, who had moved from banking to the Bethlehem Steel shipyards, had ventured into Wall Street and was already a name to be considered in finance. He had to be near Wall Street, closer to the on-the-spot maneuvering and trading. He was changing his address to New York, and he was bringing his family down with him.

"Merrily we roll along, roll along, roll along . . ."

The children were singing, and Mother Kennedy joined them.

"Nobody really likes to leave a place he knows so well," she said to the children. "But we'll be closer to Dad, and he'll be home with us more."

"Merrily . . ."

"Will we be able to go swimming?" asked Jack. "Will we have a boat?"

Seven-year-old Rosemary and six-year-old Kathleen were completely involved with the passing scenery, but five-year-old Eunice wanted to know, "Will we have a lawn for football?"

She could play football almost as well as her big brother.

"We'll have a lawn," said Mother, hushing two-year-old Patricia back to sleep.

"We may not be so close to the water, but there are other things."

Joe Jr. was quiet. He was the oldest. His ties were greatest.

"We'll get to know new kids," he said at last. "We'll make new friends; don't worry about that."

"I'm not worried," said Jack.

"Everything is moving so fast," said Kathleen.

"Merrily we roll along . . . ."

Joseph Kennedy had provided a private car for his family. The train moved swiftly through Massachusetts, through Connecticut, and into New York. There is always uncertainty about a venture into a new neighborhood, a new town, a new city. There is also the excitement of anticipation.

"What kind of house are we going to live in?"

"What are the kids like?"

"New York is bigger than Boston, isn't it?"

"Merrily we roll along, roll along . . ."

"Whatever it is," said Mother Kennedy, "you're big children, and you're clever children, and you're going to get along just fine, and you're going to like it."

Their first house in New York was at 252 Street and Independence Avenue, Riverdale-on-Hudson. Later they moved to Bronxville. Joseph Kennedy was doing well. His financial ventures, his investments, were paying off magnificently, but nothing satisfied Joe Kennedy more than his investment in his family. He nurtured its every step. He delighted in its growth. More than all else, he wanted to inculcate in his children an understanding of values, not the least of which was an understanding of the value of money.

When young Jack came to him one evening, after dinner, asking, "Dad, do you think you can increase my allowance?" Joe Kennedy contained his smile and asked in turn, "And just how much is the allowance you're getting right now, my boy?"

"Forty cents a week," replied Jack, "and that isn't enough, Dad, for all my expenses."

"Expenses?" queried his father.

"I've a lot of new expenses, Dad," pleaded the young Jack.

"I'm sure," said Joe Sr. "Suppose you write me a letter about it. Tell me how much you need and just what for."

"And then will I get it?" asked Jack eagerly.

"We'll weigh the merits of your request and come to a just decision, I'm sure."

Jack set himself to the task.

"A plea for a raise by Jack Kennedy," he titled his paper. "Dedicated to my father, Mr. J. P. Kennedy. Chapter I."

Then followed the body of his argument.

"My recent allowance is 40¢," he wrote. "This I used for aeroplanes and other playthings of childhood but now I am a scout and I put away my childish things. Before I would spend 20¢ of my 40¢ allowance and in five minutes I would have empty pockets and nothing to gain and 20¢ to lose. When I am a scout I have to buy canteens, haversacks, blankets, searchlicgs poncho things that will last for years and I can always use it while I can't use chocolate marshmallow sunday ice cream and so I put in my plea for a raise

24

of thirty cents for me to buy schut things and pay my own
way around.

Finis,
John Fitzgerald Francis Kennedy"

The grammar wasn't particularly good, the spelling would
always be atrocious, but Joseph Kennedy never gave up that
letter.

There were to be many letters Joe Kennedy would store
up. He cultivated the practice of letter writing in his children, and their letters are a quick outline of the history of
their development from childhood into youth, from youth into
maturity.

"Dear Dad," wrote Jack Kennedy from the Canterbury
School.

"I landed up in the fourth group which is not so bad. . . .
I am allowed to have a victrola so if you would please
bring up one of those folding victrolas if there are any around
when you come up for Father's day if you are coming. . . .
Also would you bring some records and some choclate pie
with whipt cream in the middle. . . ."

Jack's first school had been the Dexter School, just a walk
from his Brookline home. In Riverdale he was enrolled in
the Riverdale Country School.

"He was a good student," says Harold E. (Pop) Klue,
who taught him history, "but there are some rare ones—the
boys who have a certain spark even at the age of ten or elev-
en. Jack was one of those boys."

"I came second in my class with a average of eighty four,"
Jack wrote to his father. "We had a history test and I got
ninety five the highest mark. . . ."

His grades in English were not the best, but he had a way
with words, even as a youngster, and he knew how to tell a
story.

"I went on a hike to West Point with the scouts," he wrote
home. "We saw Biff Jones up there. We then went to the
camp. We had to sleep in these small cots with no mattress
or anything and with our clothes on. You can imagine what
a nice quiet night I had."

He had as little sense for paragraphing as he had for spelling, but he knew how to ink in a character, how to drama-
tize an incident.

"We had this real tough Ass. Patrol Leader," the letter

continued, "all he said was Shut up. The next morning I burned my bacon and the quartermaster told me to cook his. I told him what had happened to mine and put in a little here and there so I did not cook his bacon and eggs. I then laced up the Ass. scoutmaster's boots, cleaned lamps, made mine and everybody else bed, Walked a mile for a coal shovel that was not needed and went for water and swept our room, I was only a tenderfoot so I had to do everything. I laced up the ass. scoutmaster's boots again I am his orderly and ran quarter of a mile for water and froze my finger so I had to have it treated. We then went to Bear mountain inn and went to-bogganing. I had two hours sleep that night. It was a nice restful enjoyable vacational hike. Not a thing to do. It was very warm (only about five below zero . . ."

When Jack was thirteen, he was enrolled at Canterbury School in New Milford, Connecticut, the only parochial school he ever attended. He got right into the swing of things and took an active part in all school affairs, especially school sports, but it was the first time he had really been away from home.

"It's a pretty good place but I was pretty home sick the first night," he wrote. "The swimming pool is great even though the football team looks pretty bad. You have a whole lot of religion and the studies are pretty hard. . . . This place is freezing at night and pretty cold in the daytime. The food is pretty good better than you get in most schools. . . .

"I got the suit the other day but I did not like the color and it was pretty itchy looking material. . . .

"Doctor Hume said he was going to write you about my right eye. I see things blury at a distance of ten feet. I can't see much color through that eye either.

"Lost two lb. when I was weighed last week . . . ."

He reserved the blood and thunder, his exploits on the playing field, for his father.

"We played Gunnery on Friday and much to my surprise I played quaterback for the whole game except three minutes. They licked us 32-0. They smeared us and the score look like it.

"One fellow was running for a touchdown and I made a flying tackle and landed him. Everybody said I played a good game. . . . One of there fellow was seventeen and when he hit you you stayed hit. One time I got him out and what a pleasure it was to see him roll and writher on the ground.

26

I was nominated Captain but . . . I could not have been (elected) because I was then on the second team."

There was a letter on the game against the Lehen Club. ". . . and it was not a sunday school picnic. You would run through their line sombody would whack you accross your face sombody else would crack your head. You would stagger, five fellows would jump on your neck. They would get you down. Then the six remaing fellows would sit on you for all sorts of reasons each one have his own paticular desire.

"They had a gentle sort of a fellow on their team called Butch. He made a cushion out of a lot of fellows and I seemed to be his most paticular desire. The score was 20-20. . . . I played pretty well. Making one touchdown and a point. . . .

"We have two more football games and it does not take much imagination to understand why I am looking forward to a pleasant week with the ground as hard as rock and two heavy teams to play. . . ."

He could evoke a scene clearly with words, and he had a ready wit. This pleased both Joe and Rose Kennedy, who read beneath the horrendous letters of complaint and the bloody tales of the wars on the gridiron that their son was having a pretty good time. His studies, however, were another matter, and the Canterbury School made it plain in a letter to his parents.

"This report is not quite so good as the last one," they wrote. "The damage was done chiefly by 'Poor' effort in Latin. . . . He can do better than this. In fact, his average should be well in the 80's."

Joe Kennedy came up to investigate.

"English . . . 86. . . . That's not bad. How do you manage it with the way you write, the way you spell?" he asked.

"I write a pretty good story, Dad."

"I know that," said Joe Sr., and cleared his voice to keep the solemnity he needed for the occasion.

"It's this Latin, Dad," said Jack.

"We'll hold that for a minute," said his father. "Mathematics . . . 95! Now that's what I call a mark! If you can get 95 in mathematics, you ought to be getting better than that in everything else. Seventy-seven in history!"

"It's rated 'Good,' Dad," protested Jack. "The average of the class is only 77."

"I don't care what the average of the class is. Why, if your Grandfather Kennedy knew you were doing so poorly in history, I don't know how ashamed he'd be."

27

"I'll do better," promised the contrite Jack.

"And religion. Only 75. And Latin! They told me my son was unusually bright. Brilliant, they said! They're wrong, or you don't like Canterbury. Which is it, son?"

Jack was chagrined. It really wasn't the worst kind of report card. He was well up at the top of the class. But he had let his father down.

"I'll get down to work, Dad. It's not the school. I know I've complained, but I like it here."

"You're not giving up swimming and football?"

"No, sir."

Jack knew how much his father enjoyed his competing in sports.

"I'll spend a little more time with my books."

"My Latin has gone up 13 points," he wrote.

"Please send me the Litary Digest, because I did not know about the Market Slump until a long time after, or a paper. Please send me some golf balls. We just finished breakfast and am going to chapel in about two minutes."

He wanted to please all the members of his family, get good grades, show his interest in history, his devotion to his religion, but abruptly his days at Canterbury were cut short.

One night, just before the Easter recess, Jack woke with a severe pain in the region of his groin.

It was only a few weeks ago that he had helped pick a schoolmate up from the snow, where he had been tumbled off his sled. They had carried the boy the long stretch back to the school, and the boy had alternately fainted and cried out about the terrific pains in his stomach. The boy had been rushed to the hospital, and an emergency operation had to be performed.

Jack's pain was not in his stomach, just a bit below and to the right, and it was bad.

The room was dark. Everyone was sleeping. He bit his lips to hold in the pain, but the pain increased, and at last he had to ask for help.

"What's the matter? What's up?"

His roommate got out of bed.

Jack couldn't speak. The pain was almost unbearable.

The roommate turned on the light.

"You're as white as a sheet!"

So was the roommate.

"Pain," Jack whispered. "Pain!" he yelled suddenly.

The boy shot out of the room, fast. The school doctor was brought to his room.

"Appendicitis," said the doctor. "It may be acute. Notify his parents immediately."

After the operation and the convalescence, it was June—too late for Jack to go back to Canterbury. It was time for the family to move out to Hyannisport, on Cape Cod, where they spent every summer.

Summer in Hyannisport meant swimming, sailing, throwing ball, good times for the whole growing family. Robert, born in 1925, and Jean, in 1928, made eight youngsters in the bustling Kennedy household, and all of them were concerned with Jack's recuperation. There was plenty of sunshine, the rolling seas, roast beef and Yorkshire pudding, chocolate pie drowned in whipped cream, and also Rosemary, Eunice and Pat to tend to his every want, whether Mother was there or not. Even Joe Jr. was solicitous.

"Are you going to join me at Choate next year?" he asked.

"I wasn't doing too badly at Canterbury," answered Jack, not too eager for the switch in schools.

"It's one of the top prep schools in the country," argued Joe.

"You go to your school and I'll go to mine," countered the recuperating Kennedy.

The rivalry between the two brothers was not emphasized that summer, due to Jack's condition, but it was there as strong as ever.

"Just because you're a big gun up there," charged Jack, "is no reason for my going."

"No. You don't have to," countered Joe, fighting to hold on to his patience. "It might be fun, though, to have my brother on the cheering squad."

It was a dig. It didn't miss. Joe was an all-around athlete, star football, baseball, and hockey player. He rowed on the Choate crew, was a top student and one of the most popular young men on the campus.

"All right, hero," said Jack. "I'll cheer you all the way from New Milford. Try hearing me when you're running the ball to the wrong goal line!"

But it was Joe Sr. who wanted Jack at Choate. He wanted his boys together.

"What's wrong with Canterbury, Dad?"

"Nothing, son. Except, I think you'll do better in Choate."

"I'll do better in Canterbury," protested Jack.

"You'll do better in Choate," said his father.

It wasn't an opinion. It was an order.

Choate it was, with brother Joe, and it was in Choate that

the fun-loving young Jack Kennedy was to earn a reputation, along with his friends, that neither his mother nor his father nor his brother dreamed possible.

"Public enemies," the headmaster of the Choate School labeled young Jack and his companions, in a moment of white hot anger. "Public enemies!"

5

Jack stepped out of church. He had awakened early this Sunday morning and hadn't waited for Joe. Besides, Joe had his own friends at Choate, and Jack didn't want to just tag along.

The air was brisk; the leaves on the trees had already changed their colors and were beginning to fall and scatter in the wind. There would be the same wind in Bronxville, the same coloring to the leaves. The girls—Kathleen, Eunice, Patricia, Jean—and Bobby would be helping with the raking, getting the lawns clean. A little homesickness, after the long summer at Hyannisport, stuck in Jack's throat, but not for long.

"You from Choate?"

It was a young, well-built boy who spoke, and he looked familiar.

"Kennedy."

"Horton."

The boys shook hands.

"This your first year?"

"Yes. Yours?"

"My first year, too."

"Big place."

"You can get lost."

They laughed.

"My name's Jack."

"Call me Ralph."

"Hungry, Ralph?"

"I can eat."

A friendship, which was to last through all their years at Choate and after, was born.

"They serve pretty good food at the Wallingford Diner."

"Ham and eggs?"

"Waffles and pancakes, anything you want."

It became a regular Sunday ritual.

The day at Choate began at seven-thirty. It was rise and shine, wash up, clean up, and rush to breakfast. Classes till lunch and after lunch till three; then compulsory athletics till half past five in the afternoon. Wash up, clean up, dinner, then chapel at seven-thirty. Back to your rooms and study. At nine-thirty, bedtime and lights out. At regular intervals each boy had his work periods. He cleaned and swept his own room and then dashed to the dining room, where he waited on tables, three times a day. There were no variations, and the housefather was there to check up on it. A school has to be well run and its schedules well kept, but it was good to get away from it all on a Sunday morning, to enjoy the comparative freedom of the town.

"What do you play?" asked Horton.

"How do you mean?"

"Football?"

"End. Backfield," said Jack.

"Your brother's a pretty good man with the ball," said Horton.

Jack began to figure he had made a mistake.

"Joe Kennedy is your brother, isn't he?" insisted Horton.

"He's my brother," said Jack, "and Choate's lucky to have him!"

By this time, Horton got the message.

"I stick pretty much to wrestling," he said, "and I play a little golf."

As a matter of fact, he was a good man on the mat, and he was one of the best golfers ever to play for Choate.

"Don't mind me," said Jack, after a moment of uncomfortable silence. "Joe and I have a little feud going. But don't get me wrong. He's my brother. And he's great! And I'm going out for the team!"

He did report for the team, but his 135 pounds placed him at a great disadvantage. The Choate players were pretty big, even for schoolboys. Jack played a great deal of football on his class team, but he was too light for the Choate varsity. It was a bitter disappointment.

"You made it!" yelled Joe, pumping his hand and slapping his back one day.

Jack had become a cheerleader.

"Well, it's better than just watching you from the stands," protested the younger Kennedy.

"It sure is," said Joe.

Then they both laughed. For all their rivalry, they were brothers as well as brothers-away-from-home. More, they were never able to lose their sense of humor for very long.

Some of this humor, however, got in the way at Choate. It

was with quite a sober face that housefather J. J. Maher wrote home:

"Jack, I feel sure, is really trying to be a better fellow, but at times the old habits are stronger than the new desire. He has been pretty consistently on time, and he has made an effort to be neat about his room—failures in that respect may be attributed to the fact that he has little idea of neatness."

A pretty shocking note this was to the Kennedy seniors, but Mr. Maher had his own little sense of humor. He appended to the note:

"But Jack is trying. And I'm sure his health is actually better for the lift even this little purposefulness has given him."

There were letters from home and promises from Jack and he didn't forget to add, "I went to mass, which lasted from 10:30 to 11:50."

Then came another note from Mr. Maher.

"I'd like to take the responsibility for Jack's constant lack of neatness about his room and person, since he lived with me. But in the matter of neatness, despite a genuine effort on Jack's part, I must confess to failure."

There is a touch of desperation here.

"Occasionally," went on Mr. Maher, "we did manage to effect a house cleaning, but it necessitated my 'dumping' everything in the room into a pile in the middle of the floor. Jack's room has throughout the year been subject to instant and unannounced inspection—it was the only way to maintain a semblance of neatness, for Jack's room was a club for his friends."

Jack had many friends, and their ideas of how to relax from their studies and other school pressures sometimes were enough to exasperate even the most patient of schoolmasters.

But there was more from Mr. Maher.

"I regard the matter of neatness," he wrote, "or lack of it on Jack's part as quite symbolic—aside from the value it has in itself—for he is casual and disorderly in almost all of his organization projects. Jack studies at the last minute, keeps appointments late, has little sense of material values, and can seldom locate his possessions.

"Despite all this," he tapered off, "Jack has had a thoroughly genuine try at being neat according to his own standards and he has been almost religiously on time throughout the Quarter.

"I believe Jack began to sense the fitness of things after

33

the midwinter, and has and is trying to be a more socially-minded person."

Maher's report sounded bad, but boys of fourteen and fifteen don't generally devote their lives to neatness and order, and both Rose and Joe Kennedy knew their son Jack would, sooner or later, buckle down to some serious work at school.

Reassuring his parents of his interest in history, in geography, in current affairs, Jack wrote, "Sir William Grenfell came today and lectured on Labrator. It was very good. I received Communion this morning and am going to Church on tuesday. I received the prayer-book and would you please send me a puff because it is very cold." He added, "Please excuse all misprints and spelling."

"I am giving up the tuck (sweet) shop for Lent," he wrote home to let his parents know he was not slipping in the ways of the Church.

"Somebody stepped on my glasses and broke the lens," he wrote to his mother. "I have put on some weight. I sank to the sixth group in my studies. They have put in two bowling alleys, ping pong tables, deck tennis and shuffleboard in the gym."

"Things are going pretty well up here," he wrote again. "We are up on Mr. Maher's corridor, right next to him, and everything we say, he bobs in and adds his comments. We are practically rooming with him, which is more than we bargained for."

In another letter home, Jack reported on a class picnic with Cappy Lineback, one of Choate's most popular house-fathers. He told of winning a pie-eating contest. The trick in the contest was to eat the pie without using your hands, and Jack won easily. After the pie-eating contest, he wrote, "Cappy bet me that I couldn't place a dime on my forehead and drop it into a funnel which was placed in my belt. I put my head back to put the dime on it and Cappy poured a glass of water down the funnel. Of course that went over big with the fellows and they howled their heads off."

There was a different kind of howling on the part of the Choate authorities at the antics of Jack and his two close friends and roommates, Ralph (or Rip) Horton and LeMoyne (or Les) Billings, who were past masters in the art of mischief.

The roommates were joined by a number of other boys: John Morse, Bob Beach, Maure Shea, Smokey Wilde, Ira Meehan, and they formed a club they called the Muckers.

The object of the club, the boys announced, was "to put over festivities in our own little way, and to buck the system more effectively."

"Time," said Jack, exactly ten minutes after all the lights were out in the dormitory. It was nine-forty.

"Time," said Rip.

"Time," said Billings.

"Time," said Beach and the rest of the Muckers.

Jack opened the door quietly.

"All clear," he announced.

"No one in sight," said Rip, as he followed Jack into the hall.

"Not even a mouse," added Les. "Hush!"

Down they went on their hands and knees, crawling past the housemaster's room.

"Up she goes," said Jack, raising a window slowly, quietly.

"And out we go," said Rip, following Jack through the window and out onto the lawn.

"Let's!" said Les, making it three, and off they went to the village candy shop.

"I'll have a chocolate soda with vanilla cream."

"Make mine a banana split with plenty of whipped cream."

"How about chocolate pie? Nothing like chocolate pie smothered with that white stuff to feed the hungry soul!"

They bought chocolates to put in their pockets and eat on the way back to school, and they climbed back in through the window.

"Quiet," said Rip, as Jack lowered it after them.

"Quiet," said Les.

"Quiet, indeed!" said the housefather, greeting the "scoundrels."

There was a stern lecture from the headmaster and a letter to three homes, and yet they did it again.

The three "Muckers," as they labeled themselves, proved to be quite a handful for anyone who tried to discipline them.

"By the time I'm thirty," announced Jack one night, long after curfew, "I'll be a $10,000-a-year man. We'll all be $10,000-a-year men," he added generously.

"You?" said Rip Horton. "Yes. I'll be a $20,000-a-year man. But Les Billings? Never!"

"What's the matter with me?" asked Billings, looking up from his math book.

"Who's going to pay a clown like you that kind of legal tender?" asked Rip in very professorial tones.

"Why, you muscle-bound funny man," said Les, hurling the book at his critic. "The only thing you'll be able to do is to sell tickets for the fat lady in a country circus!"

"Says you," said Rip ducking the book, picking up a pillow, smacking it across the room, and hurling Les Billings off his chair.

"Says I," said Les, picking himself up from the floor and moving directly into the combat area.

In seconds, the three of them were involved, Jack, as well as Les and Rip; and in no time at all the room was a shambles.

"What are you Muckers doing now?" demanded the housefather, pushing open the door of their room.

"Practicing," said Les.

"Restaging the Battle of the Marne," said Rip.

"A debate," said Jack.

There was another session with the headmaster, another letter home.

Finally the headmaster of Choate, Mr. St. John, reached the end of his patience.

The whole school was at chapel, seated and quiet.

"Boys," the headmaster began, "I should like to tell you the story of the bad apple."

He was looking directly at the Muckers particularly Les Billings, Rip Horton, and Jack Kennedy. The boys did not stir in their seats.

"You all know," continued the headmaster, "how close and tightly packed apples are in a barrel. One bad apple can spoil the entire barrel!"

He stopped for a moment to let the meaning of his words sink in. He didn't need to wait that moment. Everyone knew what he was talking about and who it was he meant. All Choate kept its eyes front and away from the culprits.

"Here at Choate," said the headmaster vigorously, "we have several of those bad apples."

He scanned his audience.

"We have a group of boys," he went on, "who deliberately and contrary to the good of the student body, have formed a club. They call themselves the Muckers! And I believe that these boys, members of this organization they call the Muckers, are deliberately trying to change the good order of things at Choate for their own amusement and their own selfish willfulness.

"Now I am certainly not going to allow such an organization to continue at Choate. I have already written to the par-

36

ents of these boys. I will speak with them and I will tell them simply that, unless this club is disbanded, unless their sons give evidence, strong evidence of a change in ways, unless their sons become students in the tradition of Choate, they shall be summarily expelled from the school. We have no place in Choate for these Public Enemies."

"St. John means it," said Les.

He was frightened.

"My dad isn't going to like this," said Rip.

"It was all in fun, Dad," said Jack to his father when Joe Sr. arrived on the scene. "We meant no harm. I guess we carried our activities a bit too far."

The Muckers had reached the end of their history, but it was a youthful episode they never forgot.

And there were other episodes in Choate not to be forgotten by Jack. There were his two years as business manager of the yearbook, *The Brief.* There was his part in campaigning for the schoolboy vote for Roosevelt against Hoover. However, Hoover took Choate by 483 votes to 115. Of course the ballot was not tallied in the national election for the presidency, but it was Jack's first experience with political campaigning. He would remember it.

He would remember also the school dances, the hours the boys talked about which girl to ask and which girl might accept an invitation.

"Who'd want to be seen with an ape like you?"

"I'm not that bad-looking, am I?"

"It makes me cry to tell you."

Schooling is more than just the grades a boy gets in his studies. Jack Kennedy's scholastic record at Choate was not brilliant. But there was the business of learning how to live with others—how to get along with his peers and with more mature people, how to serve both his friends and his community.

"You wouldn't expect it from a fellow who was so disorganized and bent on having a good time," said Les Billings, "but Jack was an amazingly good business manager of *The Brief,* Choate's yearbook. He sold an awful lot of ads for it."

"He was always welcome in our home," said Cappy Lineback, "and he was a regular for Mrs. Lineback's waffles every Sunday night."

He made friends quickly, with both young and old. He earned their respect, as he respected them. For the first time he became aware, and he was made aware, of his own possibilities.

"How come you know so much?" asked Rip, as Jack tossed off one answer after another while they listened to the then most popular radio program, "Information Please."

"How do you remember all those details?" asked Les Billings as Jack reeled off a series of names and dates and places.

"Are you serious?" queried Jack.

"Sure, I'm serious."

"Well," began Jack, "I guess it's just that I read an awful lot of the time and think over carefully what I've read."

He would continue to impress people with his remarkable memory for facts and figures. He would also develop in an area first pointed up for him by his English instructor at Choate, Harold Tinker.

"Your penmanship could certainly take a bit of improving," said Mr. Tinker, "but you've got a gift in your pen."

The older man studied the boy.

"I think you've got the makings of a writer in you," he said, "if you ever take it seriously enough."

There would come a time when young Jack Kennedy would remember the words of Harold Tinker. There would come a time when Jack Kennedy would take seriously the gift of writing. There would even come a time when his penmanship would improve. But in his last months at Choate, Jack was more preoccupied with what college he was going to enter in the fall.

"You're going to apply to Harvard, I suppose," said Joe Kennedy, Sr., as the important day drew near. "I presume Harvard is the college you'll be wanting to attend."

Harvard was Joe Sr.'s alma mater. Joe Jr. was completing his sophomore year there. He was making a great name for himself, scholastically and athletically. It was quite natural for Joe Kennedy, Sr., to expect Jack would follow suit.

"I'd like a little time to think about it," said Jack.

"How is that?" asked the surprised Joe Sr.

"I'm not sure," demurred Jack.

"It was good enough for me. It has been good enough for Joe. You had better make up your mind and get your application in before the week is up. Those classes get filled up mighty fast. Unless you have some other school you'd prefer to my alma mater."

Jack took a couple of precious days, then broke the news.

"I'm going to Princeton, Dad."

"If that's what you want."

Joe Sr. didn't hide his disappointment.

"You want to get away from your brother, I take it. Too much competition."

"It's not that, Dad," offered Jack. "Les Billings is going to Princeton. So is Rip Horton. We've been good friends."

"You don't go to a school because your friends are going there," lectured Joe Sr. "That isn't the real reason, is it?"

"I'm not sure why I want to go to Princeton," said Jack, "but I do know I want to go there, unless you're that much set against it."

"It's your schooling," answered Joe Sr. quietly, "and your choice. I have always believed, and you know it, that you, that Joe, that all my children, should develop a sense of independence and an ability to act on their own. You don't need to argue Princeton to me. I know its reputation. I'm sure it's as good as Harvard or Yale. You want to go there. I can be disappointed, and I can get over my disappointment. You go ahead to Princeton."

So it was settled. For once Jack was not going to follow after his brother.

"You'll be glad you sent me to Princeton," said Jack soberly. "I'll make you proud of me."

It wasn't easy for Jack to move against the express wishes of his father, to hurt him even this little. But he had come to his own decision, and he would carry it through.

"Just do what you can," said Joe Sr. "You've got enough on the ball. Just do your best. That will be pleasing to me any time and all the time."

There was a summer to be spent on the Cape before Jack left for Princeton. Rip Horton promised to visit Jack for a couple of weeks, and so did Les Billings, though not at the same time. It would be fun to see his old friends, the ex-Muckers, the ex-Public Enemies again.

And it was, but only for a brief few days.

★ ★
6
★ ★

"Up, Rip!"

Jack snapped the blanket off his bed.

"What? Who?" The startled Rip Horton blinked.

"Up and at 'em!" whipped Jack Kennedy. "The sun's in the heavens and the bacon's on the fire!"

"Are you crazy?" Horton scowled, trying to retrieve his blanket.

"All the world is mad except for Rip Horton, but it won't be long and he'll join us. Up, you sleeping beauty! Up!"

"Come on now, Jack," pleaded Rip, turning his face to the wall. "Let a fellow get some sleep."

"Seven-thirty and all is well," intoned his tormentor. "Rise and shine, you Mucker! Rise and shine!"

"Go shine yourself," responded Rip. "I'm not getting up in the middle of the night."

Jack grabbed the pillow from under the groggy head of his friend and whacked him with it.

"That's the newest kind of alarm clock you can buy," announced Jack. "We've got the latest in everything around here."

"You want to fight?" challenged Rip, snatching the pillow out of Jack's hands.

Jack retreated far enough to get Rip out of bed.

"The bacon and eggs are on the table," he said. "I'm going to get mine before they're all gone. I'll mess with you later."

"Why in heaven do you have to eat so early on this blessed Cape of yours?" wailed Rip.

"Routine, Rip. They're all marching down to the dining room right now. Coming?"

Rip was resigned.

"Maybe I should have joined the Army. They pay you for getting up early in the Army."

"It's the Navy here in Hyannisport," corrected Jack. "Better get moving if you expect anything left at mess."

Rip tossed the pillow at Jack's head.

Jack caught it.

"No place to run this ball in this room," he said. "Go take your shower!"

"And you're as clean as a new-born babe, I suppose. Go fix your mop of hair. I'll be out of the shower before it's combed."

He was, too.

There were six different bottles of hair tonic in the medicine chest. Jack had tested them all, and they were all equally useless when it came to controlling his thick and bushy crop of hair.

"Stay back!" he ordered.

It never did.

He was eighteen, now, tall and lean, with a narrow face and a snub nose.

"Joe's better looking," he admitted to himself in the mirror, "but I wouldn't be half bad if I could only get this mop up and away from my forehead."

He pulled the comb through it; he pushed the brush through it.

"I'll have to invent some kind of grease," he said, battling the losing battle. "Or else I'll shave it all off!"

"A good idea," said Rip Horton, coming out of his shower. "Why don't you shave it off and join some lonely brotherhood?"

The bottle of hair tonic was poised in Jack's hand.

"Not that," pleaded Rip. "Not that!"

"You'd get all six of them," said Jack, his hand itching at the temptation, "except I can still smell the bacon. That's a good sign. There must be a strip or two no one has seen yet. Let's go!"

"And you're going to take all that hair with you?"

"Do you want to eat?" asked Jack. "Or do I have to duck you in the shower?"

"I want to eat," said Rip, moving fast into his clothes. "Let's!"

As Jack had warned, the Kennedys were already at breakfast, Dad, Mother, Joe, Rosemary, Kathleen, Eunice, Pat, Robert, Jean, and even the smallest of them all, Teddy.

"Early to rise, the early bird. We all start the day with the sun," said Jack.

"Not at Choate, you didn't," said Rip, "if you could help it."

"We're not at Choate," said Jack. "We're in Hyannisport. Your top behavior now!"

"Good morning."

"Good morning."

41

"Good morning."

Joe Kennedy, Sr., rose to welcome the visitor, to shake his hand. "I'm sorry I wasn't home to greet you last night," he said.

"Thank you, sir," said Rip, a bit overwhelmed by the warmth of the older man, a legend among the boys at school, as well as a legend in Wall Street and Hollywood, where he had become one of the more important producers of big pictures, and all points in between. "It's good to see you again."

"You're the man who handles the golf clubs like a pro," said Kennedy, Sr.

"Rumor, sir. Rumors," said Horton modestly.

"We'll put those rumors to the test sometime soon," said Joe Kennedy, Sr., "if you don't mind playing with an amateur."

They would play together, and many times more in the years to come.

"Sit down and help yourself," said Joe Kennedy, Sr.

"Dig in before Joe eats it all," said Jack, reaching for a glass of milk.

"There's more of everything," said Kathleen. "Don't let Jack hurry you."

"He's the one likely to eat it all," said Pat, buttering a hot biscuit.

"That's your fifth," said Rosemary to Pat. "Watch you don't put on too much weight."

"Look who's talking!" Jean bantered.

But there was plenty of everything for everyone, and especially there was plenty of milk. The Kennedys loved milk, still do, and there were eleven Kennedys at that table.

Tom Schriber, who was also visiting the Kennedys, sat quietly contemplating the last hot cake on his plate.

"You're not very hungry today," said Rose Kennedy, looking over at the young man who was visiting her son Joe.

"After four eggs and a rasher of bacon, I guess I'm not." He sighed.

"See what you missed, Rip!" scolded Jack. "The bacon is all gone!"

"There'll be more coming," said Mother Kennedy. "Don't you worry, Rip. You need a hearty breakfast for the routine in this household."

Rip looked at Jack inquiringly, and Jack nodded his head solemnly.

"No rest for the weary in Hyannisport," he said. "Gird your muscles. First thing on the program, right after breakfast, sailing. My boat today, Joe?" he asked, turning to his brother.

"Sure you want to go out today?" asked Joe, an odd doubt in his voice.

"You can stay home if you want to," snapped Jack. "We're sailing the *Victura*."

"O.K. with me," came back Joe quickly. "We'll go along, won't we, Thomas?"

Tom began to protest, but Joe Jr. interrupted him.

"You want to see how Jack skippers his boat, don't you?"

"Of course. Of course."

Neither Joe Sr. nor Rose interfered with such discussions, plans, or differences.

"Just be sure to get back in time for calisthenics," said Joe Sr.

"Calisthenics?" asked Rip Horton.

"Routine," said Jack. "Instructor and all."

Rip thought of what he had said about the Army, but he said nothing.

"Then there's swimming instruction and football, touch football," added Jack, slowly spelling out the routine, enjoying all the while the silent suffering of his friend.

"And we all play touch football," chimed in Eunice.

"All of us," said Pat.

"All of us," added Bobby.

Rip looked at Joe Kennedy, Sr., a man who had made millions on Wall Street and in the moving picture industry, who had been one of the top men in the drive to win the presidential election for Franklin Delano Roosevelt, the man F.D.R. had appointed the first head of the then new Securities and Exchange Commission, who was to head the Maritime Commission and become the United States Ambassador to Great Britain.

"You, too, Mr. Kennedy? Calisthenics? Swimming? Touch football?"

"And golf, too, if you're not too tired, Rip."

"Yes, sir!" said Rip, and he dug into a hearty breakfast. The day had begun.

Once aboard the *Victura*, the boys began to discuss college.

"Dad tells me you're going to Princeton," Joe Jr. said to Jack.

"That's right," said Jack.

"You, too?" Joe asked Rip.

"Is there anywhere else?" answered young Horton.

43

"Of course not," said Joe. "You Tigers run the boat. Come on, Tom. We'll take it easy down below."

It wasn't like Joe to go below deck when he was out on a boat, and Jack was suspicious, but he was mad, too.

"Crimson, down below, you lubbers!" he ordered. "Tiger, up with the mainsail!"

"Up she goes!" yelled Horton, pulling on the rope.

"Jib!"

"Jib!"

"We'll show them!" challenged Jack.

"Up Princeton!" shouted Rip to the wind, to the water, to the men in the cabin, to anybody who would hear him. "Up the Tiger!"

The wind caught the sails, and Jack piloted the boat gently out into the sound.

" 'Yo-ho-ho, and a bottle of rum!' " sang Rip Horton.

" 'Pieces of eight!' " shouted Jack.

"Not a galleon in sight," said Rip. "My arms ache for the gallant ladies."

"And the gallant gold," added Jack.

" 'Yo-ho-ho, and a bottle of rum!' "

"Is that a cloud I see in the skies, matey?" asked Rip Horton.

They were a good hour out of port.

"It's coming up fast," said Jack.

"Squall?" asked Rip.

"We get them out here once in a while," said Jack. "Good thing you can swim."

"I wouldn't like to swim in a squall," said Rip.

"Neither would I," said Jack. "Hold fast now! Here she comes!"

"Wow!" yelled Rip, as the rain came fast and furious.

"Watch the boom!" shouted Jack.

"How about Joe and Tom?" asked Horton.

"What about them?"

"They could help, couldn't they?"

"Not while I'm piloting this ship!"

"As you say, Skipper!"

"He knew it was coming!"

"Who?"

"Joe! That's why we're running the boat! That's why he's down below! Head down!" yelled Jack.

"Almost got me that time," said Rip, carefully looking up. "Which way do we go?"

"Home," said Jack. "Home. If we can make it."

"You're not sure."

"I said it was lucky you could swim."

"I said I'd rather not," reminded Rip Horton.

"Neither would I," said Jack.

But he was a good pilot. He knew his boat. He knew how to handle her. And the squall and the rain were over before Hyannisport came back onto the horizon.

"Wet up there?" yelled the very dry Joe Kennedy, Jr.

"As a hen!" came back Rip.

"Why didn't you wear your slickers?" joined in Tom Schriber.

"A good skipper studies his weather charts and listens to the late weather reports," said Joe Jr., playing at being father again.

"And a good brother sees to it that his brother gets soaked to the skin, learning all about it," said Jack.

"You're not going to let a little rain water get you mad at me, are you?"

Jack frowned. He took one good look at Rip.

"Boy, you sure are a drip," he said.

"Drop-drop," said Rip. " 'Yo-ho-ho, and a bottle of rum!' "

" 'Pieces of eight,' " added Jack, and he laughed, and Rip laughed.

"Next time, you!" said Jack, pointing his finger at Joe.

"Make him walk the plank," contributed Tom Schriber.

"That's an order!" yelled Rip.

And they were all laughing and chasing each other across the wide lawn to the house.

" 'Yo-ho-ho, and a bottle of rum!' "

Time for lunch!

Time for calisthenics.

Everything went at a pace in the Kennedy establishment.

Time for swimming.

Ten-year-old Bobby Kennedy edged away from the pool, turned and slowly began to walk away.

"Where are you going?" shouted Pat.

"Bobby!" commanded his father.

"Yes, Dad?"

"Swimming instructions."

"I wanted to fix my new plane, the one you brought me from Washington. I thought I could fly the plane for a while, Dad."

"The kit can wait, can't it?"

"I guess so, Dad."

Bobby moved back to the pool, with Eunice and Rosemary and Kathleen, the whole Kennedy clan and its guests.

"Everybody goes swimming, son," said Joe Sr. "Everybody takes his swimming instructions."

It was the one sport in which Jack was better than his brother Joe, and he was never reluctant to demonstrate his superiority.

"How about it?" he asked, pointing at the other side of the pool to his brother.

"Going to race?" asked Kick excitedly.

She never tired of her brothers' rivalry.

"Sure thing!" announced Joe.

He turned to Jack.

"Beat you this time!" he challenged.

He was challenging the champion.

"Race! Race!" yelled Jean delightedly.

"On your mark!" announced Rosemary. "Set! Go!"

Into the water plunged the two swimmers, skimming the surface.

"Go it, Jack!" yelled Kick.

"Go it, Joe!" yelled Eunice.

"Go it! Go it!" yelled the younger Kennedys.

Stroke and stroke, the steady trip-trip of their feet churning up the water behind them, brother and brother, neck and neck.

"Go, Joe!" shouted Eunice.

"Go, Jack!" shouted Kick.

"Go! Go!" yelled the younger viewers.

Then slowly, imperceptibly at first, Jack forged ahead.

"Go, Jack!" It was Kick and Pat.

"Get him, Joe!" It was Eunice and Bobby.

The easy rhythm, the sure, strong stroke; Jack pulled out five, ten, fifteen yards, and up and out of the pool!

"The winner!" announced Rosemary, raising his right hand.

"Next time, Joe! Next time!" consoled Eunice.

"Next time, maybe!" said Jack.

Swimming was his department, and he crowed, as he might, over his victory. No one watching that race in Hyannisport, however, could know that summer how much the swimming at Cape Cod would mean to Jack Kennedy in only a few short years.

"Dinner!" announced Rose Kennedy, breaking into the celebration.

"And am I starved!" said Rip Horton.

"I'm glad you are," said Rose Kennedy, smiling.

"Watch your manners," said Jack. "We're likely to have an ambassador or a senator or some secretary of something eating with us."

"Or all three," said Joe.

"I'll out-eat all of them," said Rip Horton.

The table at the Kennedys was always well set and well crowded, as it had been from the very beginning, and the table talk centered on the affairs of the city, the state, the nation, the world.

Tom Schriber had been there before, but this was Rip Horton's first dinner with the Kennedys, and he listened in amazement.

"Don't you think, Dad, there should be stronger controls on the use of the airways by the radio corporations?" asked Joe, helping himself to a full platter of steak and potatoes.

"Has the Tennessee Valley Authority really cut into the private manufacture of power to any great extent?" asked Kathleen, passing the plate of green vegetables to Rip Horton.

"This Adolf Hitler is more than noise. He's a threat. His program means war," pronounced Eunice.

Question, answer, debate; this came as part and parcel of the dinner, from soup to dessert.

"It's amazing the way you fellows talk up to your father. I don't mean with any disrespect," said Rip Horton later, scratching his head to emphasize his admiration for the give-and-take in the Kennedy family. "I mean the way he listens to you talk out your ideas, argue them, weigh them. What do you fellows know about these things when you come up against your father?"

"We talk," said Jack. "Dad has always encouraged it. Thinks we ought to develop our own ideas, our own points of view, and learn to fight for them."

"I've got to take my hat off to him," said Rip. "And I bet he's a good man on that golf course, too."

"He'll give you a battle all the way," said Jack.

There is nothing like the admiration of an outsider to make a son more aware, more proud of his father.

"He doesn't lose easily," said Jack.

He thought for a moment.

"You know," he added quietly, "Dad was set on my going to Harvard."

"Hah!" cut in Rip. "That's one battle he lost!"

"It's the first I ever won," said Jack meditatively. "And if it weren't for you and Billings, you old Mucker," he added, slapping the back of his old partner in "crime," "I wouldn't

47

be too sure about that, either. Dad doesn't make mistakes too often. As a matter of fact, I can't remember his ever making a mistake."

Jack was puzzled, and yet, later that very evening, he would battle again against a decision his father had made for him.

7

They were alone in the living room, Joseph Kennedy, Sr., Rose Kennedy, Jack. The younger children had retired. Joe had walked down to the water's edge with the guests of the house. Jack had been reading an article on Hitler's rearming of Germany.

"Isn't it a violation of the Versailles Treaty, Dad?" he asked.

"A clear violation," affirmed his father.

"Why isn't something done about it? With all his big speeches about the one-thousand-year Reich, and the war club he's waving around, what are the French doing about it? What are the English doing about it?"

"What is the United States doing about it?" countered Kennedy Sr.

"Nothing," said Jack after a moment.

"What should we do about it?" pressed Joe Sr.

"I'm not sure," said Jack. "Isn't he a threat to the peace of the world?"

"I imagine he is very much a threat to the peace," contributed Rose Kennedy. "If the League of Nations had ever been what Woodrow Wilson wanted it, there might have been someone or something to check him."

"Do we go to war to stop him?" asked Kennedy Sr. "What would you do if you were President of the United States?"

"I'm not sure," said Jack thoughtfully. "I don't think I know enough to answer that one, Dad."

He turned back to the article he had been reading, but the discussion had led to where Joe Kennedy knew it would sooner or later. Jack had given him the lead, and he took advantage of it.

"How about getting a little firsthand knowledge of the enemy, Jack?" he asked.

"Hitler's not our enemy," came back Jack, a little puzzled. "Not yet, anyway."

"No. Not yet," agreed his father. "I wasn't thinking of Hitler, nor of Stalin, for that matter. As a matter of fact, it's not the external enemy I had in mind as much as the opponent, the opponent at home and the opponent abroad."

"How do you mean that, Dad?"

"That should be clear to you, Jack," said his mother. "Men and women who oppose the program you think best for your country, for the whole world."

She knew where Joe Sr. was leading. She lent him a hand.

"You mean the Republican platform, high tariff, and all that. We went over all that in school," protested Jack.

"You learned precious little about the socialists, I'll wager," said his father.

Jack finally got the drift of the conversation. He knew what his father had in mind, and he wasn't sure that he liked it.

"We'll get all that at Princeton," he hedged.

"You'll do better in London with Professor Laski," said Joe Sr. "He's a brilliant man, though you know I don't hold at all with his theories. You can learn a great deal from him. You'll have to be alert every minute of the time you're with him. It'll call on everything you have and some more, everything you've learned and understand and believe in, to battle against the ideas he'll try to teach you."

"And when am I supposed to do all this?" asked Jack.

He was stalling for time, and his father knew it. You let the rope out a little before you pull in the line.

"This summer," he said.

"You mean that you want me to go to London this summer, just to study with someone I'm not supposed to take seriously?"

"I never said that you're not to take him seriously. On the contrary, you're to take him most seriously. I know. I know. I've been told a thousand times if I've been told once. How is it that a man whose heart and soul is in free enterprise sends his sons to be educated by a man who is completely opposed to it? You'll never understand the position of these people better, Jack; you'll never understand the communists better, either, than after a summer with Harold Laski at his London School of Economics. Take my word for it. I didn't steer Joe wrong, sending him there. Ask him. I'll never steer you wrong, Jack."

"It's not that, Dad," demurred Jack.

He knew his case was hopelessly lost, but he had to try.

"It's not what, Jack?"

"I'd looked forward to a summer on the Cape, the boats, the swimming, the girls."

"You can sail right outside of London, and you'll have plenty of time for it," said Joe Sr.

"And there'll be lots of pretty girls in London," added Rose.

"At the London School of Economics?" asked Jack. "I can picture them!"

But his argument was weak. He knew it. He smiled at his defeat.

"You won't be sorry, son," said his determined father. "You might be unsure at first. This Laski is quick and sharp, and his arguments are going to sound convincing. You'll be confused. He'll have you believing everything that he believes, for a while."

"Sounds dangerous," said Jack.

"Only if you don't think!" countered Joe Sr. "And my boys have been born and trained to think!"

"I hope so, Dad."

"I know so. And your mother knows so. Sometimes, Jack, I think we have more confidence in you than you have in yourself. You're a Kennedy, and the son of Joe and Rose Kennedy. And we both believe, your mother and I, that one has to fight for his place in the sun, for his birthright, for the country that gave him birth, and for all its great traditions, all its heritage."

"I'm with you there, Dad," said Jack quietly.

When Joe Kennedy, Sr., wanted something done, he went all out to do it; he pulled out all the stops. He expected his boys to do no less, and Jack knew it.

"You'll be competing against a master," continued Joe. "It's easy enough to beat a strawman. Learn how to battle, son, fighting a real opponent. It's the same in the world of ideas as it is in the world of sports; except that maybe in the world of ideas the stakes and the battles are a whole lot tougher."

"I'll battle," said Jack.

He didn't know how, but he knew he would do it, if only for his father.

"Of course," said Joe Sr. "I've already enrolled you at the school. And your passage is booked."

Jack couldn't help laughing.

"Did you ever lose even so much as a skirmish, Dad?"

"With your mother," said Kennedy Sr.

"When?" asked Rose, trying to recall.

And they all laughed.

"I suppose I'll be needing some clothes, Mother," said Jack.

"That's been arranged, too," said Rose, smiling her nicest smile. "We're going to the tailor in the morning."

Joe Kennedy, Jr., was the young man slated for a career in politics. Joe Sr. and Rose, both, looked to Joe Jr. to carry on the tradition of the Kennedys and the Fitzgeralds. The boys' grandfathers had limited their political activities principally to Boston and the state of Massachusetts. Joe Kennedy, Sr., had been prominent in the campaign to elect Franklin Delano Roosevelt to the country's presidency and had accepted offices of national obligation and responsibility from the President. How far Joe Jr. would go in the political arena was a moot question, but there was no doubt in the Kennedy family about the direction of their first son's ambitions.

"They wouldn't take Al Smith," said Joe Sr. "The country wasn't ready for the election of a Catholic to the presidency. Maybe Joe Jr. will be the man to break that barrier. At least, I'd like to see him try."

It would take tragedy and the passage of years before those political hopes would turn to their second-born son.

Meanwhile, "Whatever field you enter, son," Joe Sr. said to Jack, "whether it's writing, or teaching, as you sometimes say, or business, or any one of the other professions, there's nothing like broadening the base of your experience. Learn what other people think. Learn what other people say. Learn how other people fight for their ideas, as well as for the material things in life. Learn how to battle against them, if need be. Learn. Learn. Learn."

Jack entered Laski's school in London. He wasn't averse to learning. He had actually keyed himself to the impending battle. It was all intellectual, of course. Jack had no idea, when he thought of a career, that his life would some day become completely bound up in politics.

Nor did Professor Laski.

"You're Joe Kennedy's brother," he said, greeting the young man. "He was quite a student. I suppose you'll be every bit as argumentative as he was."

"I hope so, sir," replied Jack, and for once the hackles of his back didn't go up at the comparison with his friend, his rival, his brother.

"Good," said Mr. Laski. "Perhaps I'll be able to convince one Kennedy."

He never had the chance. Jack was hardly settled in London before his skin developed a severe itch.

At first he thought it might be the wool of his suit. It was

52

a warm summer. Then he thought it might be the food or the change in climate. It was neither.

Then he noticed an alarming symptom while looking in his mirror.

He blinked his eyes and rubbed them. The mirror showed clearly that the whites of his eyes were discolored.

His hands had begun to turn yellow, and his face, too.

"Jaundice," the doctor said.

Three thousand miles is a long way from home when you are ill.

"What do I do, Doctor?"

"I think you ought to go into the hospital. Have you any family here?"

"None," said Jack.

"Then the hospital is the only place for you."

"Except home. I'd like to get home as soon as I can," said Jack.

He knew no one could give him the kind of care he would get from his family. As soon as the doctor permitted him to travel, he left London for Hyannisport.

He was a pretty sick young man, and the summer was gone before he was well again. Even then, he wasn't quite finished with the disorder that had struck so suddenly; it was to return at another crucial moment in his life.

Late in August of that year, Grandpa Honey Fitz paid an unexpected visit to his recuperating grandson.

"And what are you doing, lounging around in the shade here, when you should be running the boats out against the winds?"

"And what are you doing here," countered Jack, grasping his grandfather's outstretched hand, "when you're supposed to be bussing all those beautiful senoritas down South America way?"

Honey Fitz had been sent by President Roosevelt on a good-will tour, and he had "Sweet Adeline-d" himself the length and breadth of the Southern continent.

"And how did they ever understand that blarney you speak for English?" asked Jack.

"You must be all well and strong again to be ribbing your old grandfather this way," chided Honey.

"Almost as well and as strong as the best vote-getter Boston ever delivered to the Democratic party."

"Is it voting you're thinking about now when you should be thinking of girls and school?"

"I'm thinking that in just three years I'm going to cast my

first vote," said Jack. "And that first vote is going to be for Honey Fitz Fitzgerald. You're going to be running for something, aren't you, Grandpa? Congress? Governor? Senate?"

Honey Fitz drank it all in. This was the sweetest kind of nectar for an old grandpa.

"Don't tell me you're not going to be battling for some office, Grandpa? I couldn't take it! My first vote is going to be for Honey Fitz and for nobody else! Why I won't even go down to the polls if your name isn't on the ballot."

"Are you all through, Johnny, my boy?"

"I've had my say."

"Now I'll have mine."

"Go ahead," said Jack.

"I will," said his grandfather. "And I'm going to tell you that you've got the sweetest blarney I've ever heard roll off a man's tongue, or a boy's tongue, or anybody's tongue; and I'm thinking it's a mighty good politician you'd make yourself."

"Never as good as Honey Fitz."

"Better!"

"Nobody's as good as Honey Fitz!"

"All right! Enough of this blather!" said Honey, throwing up his hands. "We're going to see the President."

"The President?" said Jack, expecting his grandfather to wink at the joke he had just made.

"The President, I said," repeated Honey Fitz. "And I said cut the blather. We're expected in Washington tomorrow. I have tickets for the first train out in the morning."

"You're pulling my leg, Gramp," said Jack. "Now just where is it you're taking me?"

"To the President," repeated Honey Fitz a little impatiently. "Franklin Delano Roosevelt, in case you've forgotten. I think it might do a bit of good for even a young whippersnapper like yourself to be meeting with the President of these United States of America."

And to Washington they went to meet with F.D.R. in his private office. Jack's heart beat faster and faster.

"Calm yourself, my lad," said his grandfather. "He's the President of the United States, but he's a man, too. A grand man!"

"Mr. Fitzgerald. Mr. Kennedy," announced the usher.

The man in the big chair raised both his hands, and with them his voice as well.

"La Dulce Adelina . . ."

"Sweet Adeline," came back Honey, moving directly to

the big chair and the big man who sat in it. He shook his hand.

"My grandson, John Fitzgerald Kennedy, Joe Kennedy's son."

"I'm glad to meet you!" boomed the President, grasping the young man's hand.

"I'm honored, sir," said Jack, looking into the firm, strong face of Franklin Delano Roosevelt.

"So you're the grandson I've heard so much talk about," said the President.

Jack was sure it was Joe he must be talking about, but he wouldn't contradict the President. Besides, he was too busy studying and admiring the man who had pulled the country out of the worst depression in all its history.

"It's quite a grandfather you've got," said the President.

"Yes, sir," said Jack.

"So you sang 'Sweet Adeline' through all of South America," said F.D.R., turning to Honey Fitz.

"I couldn't think of a better way of reaching them. I never could speak their language. Never could speak anything but English. But music—everybody understands music."

"*La Dulce Adelina*," sang out the President.

"That's the way they sing it down there," apologized Honey.

"And a beautiful translation," said the President.

He threw back his head and laughed uproariously.

"Why, they tell me they think *La Dulce Adelina* is our national anthem," continued the President.

And again the laugh. Fitz laughed too. And Jack managed to smile. Meeting the President of the United States was too momentous an occurrence for him to laugh.

"Three years and then I can vote," he thought.

That was as far into the future as young Jack Kennedy could think that special, that wonderful afternoon.

8

"So this is the best you could do for me?" said Jack, dropping into the one overstuffed and overaged chair in the room. "I thought Princeton was one of those lush places you read about in the newspapers."

"Sorry, sir," said Les Billings. "The people who run this place haven't the vaguest idea of who it is they're entertaining. We might as well have just come off the boat."

"They don't speak English, Jack," confided Rip Horton.

"At least they don't seem to understand it."

"We asked for a rug six inches thick," put in Les.

"They just look at us."

"We asked for Louis XIV furniture, or late Georgian, or bentwood, something with a bit of distinction," added Billings, "and they give us this late Salvation Army stuff."

"We tried," said Rip.

"We told them Jack Kennedy was coming."

"They don't even know who you are."

"Barbarians."

"Savages."

"Are you comfortable, Jack?"

Jack looked around at the shabby room, the old furniture, the unpainted walls, the sad, drooping curtains on the windows.

"It's not the furnishings, gentlemen," he said. "Contrary to your carping witticisms, I find these quarters to be sumptuously decorated and in elegant, almost lavish taste. If there is a fault, and I am afraid there is, it's that I share this magnificent suite with a couple of crude and uncultured baboons!"

Les had a book in his hand. Rip picked up the lamp from the table.

"Why you . . ." began Billings, poised to hurl the first missile.

"Cease and desist!" yelled Jack, throwing up his hands.

"The Muckers are dead!"

Les dropped his book. Horton set the lamp back on the table.

"We're in Princeton," said Jack, as if he were speaking of

a sanctified temple. "A little reserve, gentlemen. A little reserve, as befits the Tiger."

But Jack couldn't be much of a tiger when he finally joined forces again with Billings and Horton.

"We don't want a recurrence of the disorder," said the doctor. "You'll have to take it easy. Good food, good hours, and a lot of rest."

"Athletics?" asked Jack. "Football? Baseball? Swimming?"

"Swimming will be all right," said the doctor, "if you're not too strenuous about it. And that's about all."

Jack had come to Princeton late, several weeks after classes had gotten under way. Billings and Horton had already settled themselves in old South Reunion, a dormitory that had seen many, many years' service. It was about all they could afford. As a matter of fact, Les Billings was stretching the little financial backing he had, even at that.

"Suits me fine," said Jack.

The room was four flights up, the bathroom in the cellar, and young Kennedy could have rented the most luxurious suite in the college, but he didn't.

He wanted to be with his friends. He wanted to be with Les and with Rip. This was what they could pay for. It was good enough for him.

It was good enough for Joe Sr., too, even though he had to stop for breath on the second landing.

"It takes more than money to make a man," he said, took off his overcoat, threw it down to his chauffeur, who was waiting on the ground floor, and proceeded to climb the heights to his son's lodgings.

"Not bad," said Joe Sr., taking a tour of the place.

"Great!" said Jack.

"And how have you been feeling?" asked Kennedy Sr.

"Right at the top!" answered his son.

It wasn't really so. The jaundice had left him woefully weak.

"Going out for the team?" asked his father.

Jack smiled.

He knew he couldn't go out for any of the sports at college. He couldn't even go out for cheer leader. He just didn't have the energy.

"I'm going to manage Rip," he said. "He's going to be the next welterweight champ."

Rip had extended his prowess in the ring to include boxing, as well as wrestling.

"He has the sweetest hook you ever saw," extolled Jack, "and the prettiest jab."

"Jab first, then hook," amended Rip.

"And then the right to keep him down for the count!" added Jack enthusiastically.

Jack kept a watchful eye on Horton, made sure he reported to the gym every day, and then put him through his paces. Jack rubbed him down before the fight, rubbed him down after the fight, yelled at him all the time he was in the ring. If he couldn't take part in a sport, the next best thing was to see that Rip turned out all right.

Rip Horton was quite good, almost as good as Jack ballyhooed him to be, but not quite.

He was a welterweight, and Jack drank in all the glory of a possible college championship; that much more glory because Rip Horton was only a freshman at the school.

"We'll win it! We'll bowl them over! We'll run them ragged!" Jack predicted on the night of the first bout.

He was as enthusiastic as any fight manager, professional or amateur, as sure as any fight manager that he had a winner.

"From what I hear about this fellow, Phil Gould," he said, working up the muscles in Rip's back, loosening them, warming them up, "you ought to be able to take him real easy."

"Sure. He's just going to lie down for me," said Rip, springing up from the rubdown table, dancing on his feet, throwing a jab at his shadow, following with a hook.

"Just keep your eye on his right hand," cautioned Jack. "They say it's murder."

"Why don't you watch it for me, Jack?" asked Rip, throwing a robe over his shoulders. "I'll go out and eat some of your chocolate pie. With loads of whipped cream."

"All right, all right," said Jack. "Turn it off. We'll eat all the pies in town if you win the championship."

"It's a deal," responded Rip, and down they walked, through the halls and into the arena, Jack massaging the back of his fighter all the way.

"I'll beat him," winked Rip, as the ten-second buzzer sounded.

"You had better!" warned Jack.

The gong sounded for the beginning of the fight.

"Go get him!" yelled Jack.

And Rip did.

His jab that night was as pretty as his manager had

58

boasted. His hook was a beautiful sight to behold. The jab kept Gould off balance. The hook landed with telling effect.

"You've got it won," said Jack between rounds, feeding Rip water, drying him with his towel. "Just keep away from his right!"

Phil Gould must have left that right in the dressing room that night, or else Rip never let him get set with it.

"The winner," announced the referee, raising the big hand of grinning Rip Horton, and Jack let out with a mighty "Tiger!"

"Let me look at you, Champ," he said in the dressing room.

"I'm not that pretty," demurred Rip. "And I'm not the champ, either."

"You will be tomorrow night!" predicted young Kennedy. "Hold your head still!"

"For what? There's nobody taking pictures."

"You've got a nick in your chin!" announced Jack.

"I must have bumped my jaw on the chest of drawers."

"Hold it! He got you there all right!"

"Where?"

"Here! Look at it yourself!"

"It's nothing at all," protested Rip, feeling for the nick that had Jack worried. "He didn't lay a glove on me."

"Nevertheless," insisted Jack, who worried about his fighter the way a mother hen fusses about her chicks, "we'll take care of it."

"There!" said Rip. "Are we all done?"

He felt the gauze and plaster Jack had used to cover the nick.

"You'd think Phil Gould won the fight, the way I'm bandaged up," complained Rip Horton.

"You've got another fight tomorrow night," countered his manager. "We're not going to give him any cuts he can open up."

"No, sir!"

"Up on your feet, man! Bill Moore tomorrow, and the championship! Let's go!"

"Let's go," repeated Rip Horton dutifully. "Where to?"

"Where to?" echoed Jack. "To get some good nourishment into you! To build up that muscle! To rack up that power!"

"Make it steak and fried onions and a heap of potatoes!" ordered Rip.

"Milk and corn flakes and lots of both!" ordered his mentor.

"Muscles? Power?" bellowed Horton.

"Corn flakes and milk!" repeated young Kennedy. "And more of the same!"

Horton followed orders. He put away the biggest dish of corn flakes and more milk than he had ever consumed in all his memory.

"If this cereal could fight," he began.

"You'll do the fighting," cut in Jack, "but this is going to help. See if it doesn't. I know something about body-building, even if you don't think so right now."

"I guess you don't know enough about it," Rip said, the night after, "about body-building, I mean."

"He was lucky!" Jack scowled, as he rubbed down his defeated contender for the welterweight honors.

Bill Moore was a little too much for the freshman battler. The jab had worked. The hook had been effective. But neither had come often enough. Moore was a clever fighter, and he had a little more experience in the ring.

"Wait till next year!" Jack declared, and Rip Horton was too tired to answer.

"You're not throwing in the towel?" challenged his manager.

Rip took a long look at the grim face of the man who was determined to make a champion of him and draped one weary arm around his shoulder.

"Jack," he asked, "do you think Johnny Harvard stands a chance to beat us?"

"What are you talking about?"

"Your brother Joe is playing football for Harvard," continued Rip, glad to get away from the boxing ring. "Who are you going to root for?"

"Princeton!" snapped Kennedy. "What do you take me for? Judas?"

"Just asking," went on Horton smoothly. "I guess your whole family will be out to see the game. Where are you going to sit?"

Jack grinned at his sore and aching friend.

"Where you sit, you big baboon!"

"And you'll wave across the field to your dad and your mother?"

"If I can see them."

He saw them between halves, and he had to practice all the diplomacy he could muster for the short reunion. After all, Joe Sr. had played for Harvard, and Jack had to be careful not to step too hard on tender territories.

The stands, of course, were jammed for the annual Princeton-Harvard classic. Fritz Crisler was coaching his Tiger squad to an undefeated, untied season, but nothing is so uncertain in the game of football as a meeting between the Ivy League rivals.

Princeton had the brilliant Jack White, Paul Pauk, Jack Kaufman, Gary LeVan, and Pepper Constable in its backfield, and Ken Sandbach to mastermind at quarterback. They had two of the fastest ends in the game in Gil Lee and Fred Ritter. Dick Weller, Alan Montgomery, and Tommy Toll made the Tiger line impenetrable. The squad had romped to a 29-6 victory over Rutgers and had overwhelmed Yale 38-7. But Harvard was undaunted.

The Crimson had its own heroes. Fred Mosely, Vernon Struck, George Ford in the backfield, and George Blackwood at quarterback. Captain Shaun Kelley and Emile Dubiel were good enough to play end for any team in the East. Burton, Gaffney, Jones, Nee, and Maser made up a formidable line. The Harvard fans let out a mighty yell as the crimson-shirted ball players ran out onto the field. They were going to stop the mighty Tiger. At least, this is what they hoped and even believed.

Jack Kennedy looked across the field. He thought he had spotted his family, but he wasn't sure. He saw his brother Joe as he came out with the big Harvard squad.

"Hey, Joe!" he yelled, and then looked around self-consciously at all the Princeton rooters surrounding him.

Joe, of course, in all the din that filled the stadium, couldn't hear him.

"Tough," said Les Billings.

"I was just saying hello to my brother," argued Jack. "That's allowed, isn't it?"

"Sure," said Rip Horton, "but I wouldn't be cheering too loud for Harvard if I were you. Not in that seat anyway."

"Who's cheering for Harvard?" growled Kennedy. "We're going to smear them all over this gridiron!"

Still, Jack couldn't take his eyes off his brother for very long. He was almost glad that Joe was still sitting on the bench when the Harvard squad trotted onto the field for the kickoff.

A mighty yell rose from both sides of the stadium as the pigskin was booted into the air. It was almost the last mighty yell for Harvard that afternoon. Princeton was just too big and too good.

The game was only four minutes old; Princeton was on the

Harvard 43-yard line. Ken Sandbach barked his signals, took the ball from his center, faked to Pepper Constable, and shoved the ball into the waiting hands of Jack White. The line made a hole for him through left tackle; that was all White needed. He was away and down along the sidelines. Ten yards, twenty, thirty. The Tiger fans were on their feet.

"Go, man! Go!"

He got away from one tackler. He got away from another. He was slowed down. They pulled him down on the Harvard three.

It was Paul Pauk who carried the ball into the end zone for the Tiger's first score. Ken Sandbach kicked the extra point. It was Princeton 7, Harvard 0.

Jack Kennedy was as rabid a rooter as the rest, but he was among the first to grow still.

He watched the Crimson line up to receive the kick-off. Joe Kennedy was still on the bench.

Harvard received, pushed the ball up to the mid-field stripe, then into Princeton territory. Struck took the ball from his center, slipped it to Fred Mosely; Mosely faded back to pass, but the Tiger ends were too fast. Gil Lee hit him hard, the ball popped out of his hands, and Fred Ritter was there to pick it up out of the air and to race down the field fifty yards, unmolested, untouched. Princeton scored again. Ken Sandbach kicked the extra point again. It was Princeton 14, Harvard 0, in the first six minutes of the ball game.

"This is a romp!" declared Les Billings.

"Two points a minute," said Rip, beginning to total up the possible final score. "That would make it 120-0. Wow!"

"Might as well tear up the goal posts now," said Les.

"Might as well," said Jack, but he could see Joe, sitting on the bench, and he knew there was no jubilation in his heart.

"They played better ball in the second quarter," said Jack to his father when they met during the mid-game ceremonies. He was searching uncomfortably for some kind of consolation.

"Don't waste any of your tears on me," said Joe Sr. "The game is only half over. Wait till the second half!"

Neither said anything about Joe, but they both wondered why he hadn't yet been used.

"Sometimes you wonder what a coach is after," said Joe Sr. And that was all.

In the third quarter, Gil Lee, playing a great game for the Tigers, blocked a punt, picked up the ball, and raced twelve yards for the third Princeton touchdown of the game. Some few minutes later, Paul Pauk returned a Harvard kick to the Crimson thirty-yard line, then took the ball over the goal line on the very next play with a brilliant thirty-yard run. Jack White scored the fifth and final touchdown for the Tigers. It was a sorry day for Harvard, a bright 35-0 victory for Fritz Crisler and Princeton.

"Too bad Joe has a bad leg. I've just heard about it," said Jack to his father after the game.

He was glad that Joe only had to watch the rout. There was some consolation for the family in that.

There was no consolation for Jack, however, in what happened only a few weeks after that memorable football game. His eyes were discolored again; his face had turned yellow.

The jaundice had returned.

"I thought I had it licked," he said.

"You went back to school too soon," said his father.

"You need a long rest," said the doctor. "You'll have to take it easy for quite a while."

"What do you suggest, Doctor?" asked the somewhat discouraged young man.

"Arizona," said the doctor. "The air is good. The climate is good. I'd take the rest of the year off if I were you."

"Doctor's orders?" asked Jack, trying to stave off the inevitable.

"Doctor's orders."

It was good-by to Princeton. He never went back.

The jaundice cleared once again, he traveled the long distance to Arizona, and in the fall, fully recuperated, Jack Kennedy enrolled in Harvard.

"It's what you want, Dad," he said, smiling quietly.

"Is it what you want, Jack?" asked Joe Sr. He wanted his son to make the decision.

"It's what I want," said Jack.

He never regretted his choice.

9

One hundred two bright and eager young men lined up for the coach of the Harvard Freshman team, Henry Lamar. Among them were some of the best football players to come out of the high school and prep school leagues of 1935. There was Tom Healy, a star baseball pitcher as well as a brilliant tackle from Worcester Academy. There was George Bailey from Exeter, Ted Holdsworth from Milton, Bart Kelly, whose brother Shaun had captained the 1935 Crimson Varsity. There was Torb MacDonald, destined to prove one of Harvard's greatest backs, and there was the six-foot lean and determined Jack Kennedy.

"All right, men," announced head coach Lamar. "You've had a soft summer. You've been taking it easy around the beaches, on your lawns. You've been keeping bad hours and grown flabby around the middle. We'll take care of all that. No smoking, no drinking, curfew, and a lot of hard work. Follow directions, keep in shape, get down on the field here and give it what you've got, and we'll have the best Freshman squad in all of Harvard's football history."

He turned to his two assistants.

"This is Joe Hill. He's my right-hand man, and he's the line coach. This is Emile Dubiel. I've borrowed him from the Varsity for a while. He's captain of your Crimson team. We're going to put you through a routine drill today. It's not going to be exciting. It's just going to be tough work and nothing else until we've whittled you down to a fighting eleven. Now let's go!"

Thirty minutes for calisthenics.

This was routine for Jack ordinarily, but now he tired too quickly and had to fight off constantly the effects of his illness and the long convalescence.

Thirty minutes around the oval, trotting, walking, running, till the wind came up hot in his throat and he was parched for something to cool the burning lining of it.

"All right, fellows!" yelled Dubiel. "Let's see a little blocking!"

They were divided into squads, the squads into elevens.

John F. Kennedy during his school years at the Choate School, Connecticut.

The Muckers at Choate, John F. Kennedy in the foreground

K. LeMoyne Billings and John F. Kennedy at Choate

A group of Choate students: (*left to right*) Ralph Horton, K. LeMoyne Billings, Charles Schreiber, and John F. Kennedy

John F. Kennedy at Choate

John F. Kennedy, 1936

The Kennedy family in their Bronxville home, 1937: (*at the left*) Joseph P. Kennedy, Sr., Patricia, and John, with Jean seated in the foreground and Eunice behind her; (*at the right*) Robert, Kathleen (seated), Edward (seated), Rosemary, Joseph Jr., and Mrs. Joseph P. Kennedy (*Bachrach Photo, courtesy of United States Information Service*)

Ambassador Joseph P. Kennedy and Mrs. Kennedy, with two of their children, John and Kathleen

Ambassador Joseph P. Kennedy in December, 1939, with two of his sons, John and Joseph Jr.

Lieutenant John F. Kennedy in the Solomons, 1943, with two fellow officers, Lieutenant Paul Fay and Ensign Leonard J. Thom, executive officer of the PT-109

Senator Kennedy and his fiancée, Jacqueline Lee Bouvier, sailing at Hyannisport, Massachusetts, June, 1953

Senator and Mrs. John F. Kennedy surrounded by relatives and friends on their wedding day, September 12, 1953: (*front row, left to right*) Hugh G. Auchincloss, Jr., Senator George Smathers, Torbert Macdonald, Benjamin Smith; (*middle row*) Edward Kennedy, Jacqueline Kennedy, Senator Kennedy, Robert F. Kennedy, James Reid; (*back row*) Michael Canfield, Charles Bartlett, Paul Fay, K. LeMoyne Billings, Joseph Gargan, R. Sargent Shriver, and Charles F. Spalding (*United States Information Service*)

Campaigning for the presidency, Senator Kennedy visits Mrs. Eleanor Roosevelt in New York City on the occasion of her seventy-sixth birthday, October 11, 1960 (*United States Information Service*)

The Democratic party's candidate for President of the United States, with Mrs. Kennedy and their daughter Caroline, at Hyannisport, 1960 (*United States Information Service*)

They tore into each other, as if they were playing the big Yale game.

"That'll be it!" bellowed Coach Lamar, as he sent them around the oval for the last run-around of the day. "We'll start the regular routine tomorrow!"

"If you can get me out of bed," someone said.

They were a very weary band of one hundred and two young, tired freshmen going back into the clubhouse.

Jack was still. He couldn't have talked if he'd wanted to. He was just too tired.

He didn't talk under the shower. He didn't talk as he slowly rubbed himself dry and began to dress. But he listened.

"Did you hear the latest?" Torb Macdonald was asking. "The latest news, of course," Torb added.

"They're scrapping the Varsity," put in Bart Kelly. "The Freshmen are going to be the big team to beat this year."

After a shower and a rubdown, the hundred and two athletes were as fresh as a spring rain and as ready to go.

"Maybe you think it's funny," countered Torb. "I don't. As a matter of fact, I don't know whether I'm coming out again tomorrow; not if what I heard has any truth in it."

"What did you hear?" asked Kelly, suddenly sober.

"What did you hear?" asked the whole locker room.

"Now I won't say it's so for a fact," hedged Torb Macdonald. "It's only what I heard."

"Open your mouth and let us have it!" ordered Tom Healy.

"Let's have it!" echoed the freshmen hopefuls, suddenly alarmed, suddenly anxious.

"Well, it's this way," began Torb slowly. "I was standing over there, near the bench, and I heard Lamar speaking to Dubiel and a couple of the other men out there."

"Yeah?" cut in Ted Holdsworth, trying to quicken the tempo of the story.

"Well, like I told you. I only heard."

"Heard what?"

"We're not going to play the Yale Freshmen this year!" announced Torb.

"What!"

The locker room exploded with rebellion.

"No Yale game, no team!"

"No Yale game, they can play without me!"

"What's a football season if we're not going to play against the Yale Freshmen!"

"Now look, fellows," pleaded Torb. "I only heard this.

You're not going to say anything about it? Somebody is going to pay for it if it leaks."

"We'll let them know!" shouted Tom Healy.

"We're not going to take it lying down!" yelled Bart Kelly.

"It isn't all that bad," said Jack Kennedy finally.

"What do you mean, it isn't that bad? It couldn't be worse if they tried!"

"Now take it easy," cautioned Jack. "We're playing Southern California instead."

"That's right," said Torb Macdonald eagerly. "That's right."

"Let them keep Southern California!"

"We want Yale!"

"You haven't heard it all, fellows," said Jack.

"Yeah?"

"We're playing them in the Polo Grounds."

"New York?" queried Bart Kelly.

"Some big scholarship thing," said Jack. "Everybody's going to be there. Benny Goodman, the King of Swing, in person, is going to lead his band around the field between halves. They're going to have the best-looking girls in the country join the parade. Hollywood stars. Bill Stern is going to do the broadcast. They're shooting the whole works."

"Doesn't sound too bad," said George Bailey.

"It's going to be a real big thing all right," said Kelly.

"Why did they pick on us instead of the Varsity?" questioned Ted Holdsworth.

"Because we're the best!" yelled Healy.

"Yeah," said the whole locker room, a little awed by the honors and the responsibilities suddenly thrust on their shoulders.

There was a silence.

Then the big booming laugh of Torb Macdonald filled the room.

"You sure are a bunch of poor, ignorant freshmen!" he shouted; and the melee was on!

Jack and Torb Macdonald, the two culprits, the hoaxers, had only their laughter to ward off the attack of wet towels, but it was enough.

"Southern California!"

"Polo Grounds!"

Then everybody was laughing, and the Yale game was still on their schedule.

"Jack Kennedy," said Jack, introducing himself to Torb Macdonald.

"You catch on quick!" said Torb, pumping the hand of his partner in crime. "Torb Macdonald's my name."

It was the beginning of a friendship that lasted through college and down through the years. Torb Macdonald, now a Congressman, is still a man to depend upon in Jack Kennedy's team.

Torb was a triple threat on the gridiron. He could kick; he could pass; he could run. He was slated to make history for Harvard's fighting elevens, to become one of its greatest backs, one of its greatest captains.

Jack was tall, six feet tall. He was a good end. He wanted to be a better one.

"How about your weight, Jack?" asked Torb.

"I'll put it on. I'll put it on."

He was too lean. He couldn't possibly take the pounding an end takes from men fifty, sixty, and seventy pounds heavier than he was.

"I'll outsmart those beefy ends," said Jack. "Let's do a little drilling on that forward pass."

Everyone else was in the showers or getting dressed. Jack and Torb were on the field, Jack working out a fancy S design down the turf and Torb throwing passes to Jack at a fixed spot.

It worked. It worked again. Again and again they worked on their pet forward-pass play.

"I've got to hand it to you," said Torb. "You pull that ball out of the air. You know how to hang on to it. You'd be the best end on any squad if you had the weight. Matter of fact, you're the best receiver I've ever seen. Just put on ten or fifteen pounds. That's all you need."

"Forget it!" snapped Jack. "Just keep pitching. This pass is going to win a couple of tight games for us!"

Torb wasn't the only one worried about Jack's weight. His brother Joe, who was playing Varsity end and who was a healthy one hundred and seventy-three pounds for his five feet eleven inches, was worried, too.

He came down into the Freshman locker room. Jack and Torb had just come in from their usual after-drill practice. Everybody else had gone.

He sat himself down next to his brother, as if he were just going to pass the time.

Torb went in for his shower. When he came out, Joe was evidently laying it on the line. Torb tried to keep out of it.

"You've just come through a serious illness," Joe was saying. "You had one relapse. Do you want another?"

Jack said nothing, but his face was red with the blood in it.

"They'll kill you out on the field there," continued Joe. "There's just too much beef for you. Do you have to play the hero?"

Jack was coming to a slow boil, but he still said nothing.

"So you don't make the team," went on Joe. "So you're not big enough to make the squad."

"He's good enough," cut in Torb. He had to defend his friend. Besides, he believed it. "He'll make the best end we've ever had, and you've no business talking the way you're talking, just because you're Varsity!"

Torb was hot under the collar himself but not as hot as Jack got.

"Mind your business!" said Jack curtly. "Keep out of it! I'm talking to Joe, not you!"

Torb shut his mouth. You don't stick your nose into a quarrel between brothers unless you want to get it flattened.

Joe, of course, had logic with him in the argument. Jack had the heart. He was going to play end for Harvard, and he did.

Playing right end in the first Freshman game of the season against Providence was one of the biggest thrills that Jack had ever had. It was Kennedy and Macdonald sparking the attack that afternoon as the Crimson boys ran over Providence. Torb ran through the Rhode Island boys' line, and when he was stopped in the line, he simply threw the ball to Jack for huge gains, as the hard-hitting frosh rolled up a 25-0 victory.

The season wore on, and the Harvard frosh team had its share of glory. Princeton was trounced by a 34-6 score. But the Army squeaked out a 7-6 win. They beat Exeter 12-7, tied Worcester Academy 6-6, and lost to Andover 6-0.

But the big thrill of the year came when Varsity coach Dick Harlow singled out Jack and Torb one day, after watching the two put on an impressive passing display in a game.

"Those two boys," said the coach of the big Crimson team. "I want to see them."

It was just a week before the Yale game, the biggest game of the year for both of the Ivy League schools.

"You've heard of Frank and Kelley, Clint Frank and Larry Kelley," said Coach Harlow to the two boys.

This was the star forward-pass combination of the Elis, the strong threat against the Crimson defense.

"Yes, sir," said Jack.

The coach hesitated a moment.

"You're pretty light, even for an end," he said to Jack.

"But he's the best receiver on the squad," put in Torb, "and once he's got the ball, he can really go."

"So I noticed," said the coach. "That's why I've got you both here."

"Yes, sir," said Torb.

"I'm going to put you in with the Varsity drills this week," said Harlow after a moment. "That is, against them!"

Both boys swallowed hard. This was a high honor. It was also going to be a buffeting, bruising honor, playing against the much heavier, more experienced Varsity squad.

"We're going to teach you the pass combinations Frank and Kelley have been using," continued the coach. "It isn't going to be easy. This Varsity isn't like anything else you've played against this year. It's a whole lot tougher and harder. They play for keeps."

Harlow looked over his boys again. He wished Jack had a little more of his brother Joe's weight, but he didn't say so.

"I expect you'll do your best," he said.

"Yes, sir," said the boys.

They walked out swiftly but quietly, then, alone, let out a wild war whoop, slapped each other on the back, and danced all the way into the locker room.

"We'll show those beef-trusters!" yelled Torb.

"I'll show them how much weight I carry," said Jack.

"Varsity, here we come!" roared Torb.

They were slightly less enthusiastic after the first workout with Harvard's big eleven.

"You'd better move a little faster," said Emile Dubiel, helping Torb Macdonald up from the hard gridiron, where he had spilled him just moments before.

Torb hadn't had time to get rid of the ball.

Jim Hallett hit him the next time, again with the ball still in his hands.

"Loosen up!" said Jack to Torb, coming back into the huddle.

"I guess I'm a bit tight," said Torb.

"And scared," said Jack.

"I'll show you who's scared!" snapped Torb.

He eluded Dubiel. Hallett was blocked out. Jack had raced twenty yards down and along the sidelines. He swerved abruptly, came in and down no more than five yards, gathered Torb's forward pass in his arms, and sprinted down the field.

"Get in there faster!" snapped Harlow, pinning back Dubiel's ears. "You don't run into a block!" he shouted at Hallett. "You cut in and away from him!"

He turned his attention to the whole Varsity.

"I've got these boys in for a purpose. This is Larry Kelley! This is Clint Frank! Stop them and we've won! And we're going to win!"

It was a tough week, as Harlow told them it would be.

"My aching bones!" said Torb, moving in for his shower.

"What bones?" asked Jack, turning on the cold water.

But they were in there, every day, as the coach had ordered. Now they would slip through the big Harvard defense. More often, it was a hard tackle, a bruising tackle, and the two freshmen picked themselves up from the gridiron more and more battered as the week went by.

Then the big game. Saturday afternoon and the stands were jammed. When Yale meets Harvard on the gridiron, the whole football world turns to watch. This is the oldest of all traditional rivalries, the Bulldog against the Crimson Johnny Harvard. Statistics, past performance, everything else goes by the boards. The two elevens come out, and for four fifteen-minute quarters it is do or die. The entire season, success or failure, depends on this one game, and everyone on the field and everyone in the stands knows it.

And this game followed the ritual, except that there were two freshmen who kept their eyes glued on Larry Kelley and Clint Frank through the greater part of the game. After all, for one week and for Harvard, they had been the two great Eli stars.

"They're as good as Harlow said they were," commented Torb Macdonald.

"Better," said Jack Kennedy.

They were good. The whole Eli squad was good. So was Harvard.

Up and down the field they struggled all afternoon. First Harvard, then Yale, taking the ball deep into each other's territory, only to be thrust back by eleven determined young men. It was a tossup as to who would emerge the victor, right from the beginning down to the last seconds of play. It had to be a glorious victory for one, a courageous defeat for the other, by the scantest of margins. It was.

The Eli partisans tore down the goal posts. Yale came off the field with the win, but Harvard could hold its head up high. The score at the end of that titanic battle was Yale 14, Harvard 13, the difference being a point after touchdown.

"We did our best," said Torb, seeking some consolation.

70

"It wasn't enough," said Jack, who would not conceal his disappointment. "We lost."

"By one point," protested Torb.

"It might just as well have been fifty," argued Jack. "No one gets medals for coming in second best!"

That's what his father, Joe Kennedy, had said to him when he was a boy.

Joe Kennedy had also said, "A man who won't alibi for losing, who doesn't enjoy losing, is more likely to end up a winner."

Jack remembered that, too. He always remembered it.

10

Jack Kennedy stretched and yawned, but he didn't get out of bed.

"What time is it?"

"Too late for breakfast."

"No!" shouted Jack.

"Yes!" shouted Torb.

They were rooming together now in Harvard's Winthrop Hall, Jack and Torb Macdonald, and this was the regular morning routine: Torb up early and ready to go, Jack taking that extra fifteen minutes under his blankets.

"See you in the dining hall."

"Hold on a minute, Torb!"

"And miss my Wheaties?"

"You won't miss a thing."

Jack was on his feet, pulling on a pair of slacks and an old sweater.

"You're too fat anyway," he said, poking fun at the good-natured Torb.

"Too fat!"

Torb punched away at the muscles of his stomach.

"Maybe," he said, "but let's make it before nine this morning. I'm hungry!"

"That's news," said Jack.

He tried to pull the comb through his thick hair, gave up, sat down again on his bed.

"Maybe you'd better go on yourself," he said.

"Something wrong?" asked Torb.

"I just don't feel like breakfast."

"You? Come on," said Torb, helping his friend to his feet. "You're going to need some of that breakfast energy if you're going to make the swim meet."

The meet was against Yale. Jack was out for a first place in the Crimson squad.

"Man's born to suffer!" He sighed, and off they went, the two inseparables, to do battle with Mrs. Dee for their breakfast.

Mrs. De Pinto, Mrs. Dee to the boys, ran her kitchen

as a mother would run her house. She was gentle and by nature most kind, but she made the rules governing her dining room and insisted that they be kept.

"It's after nine," she said. "The kitchen is closed."

"But Mrs. Dee," began Jack, looking at his watch in complete amazement.

"There's nothing wrong with the clock on the wall," cut in Mrs. Dee. "Get yourself a new alarm clock."

"But Mrs. Dee," began Jack again, "if you knew what happened to us this morning..."

"Ah!" cut in Mrs. Dee once more. "The roof fell in, the walls collapsed, and you had a hard time rescuing the old groundkeeper from underneath all the rubble. No! None of your old Irish fairy tales this morning! It's after nine, and there is no breakfast in this dining room!"

"All right, Torb," said Jack, turning to his pal. "My fault. I guess I'll have to stop writing letters to my mother first thing in the morning. Sorry, fellow."

"You're a scamp and you're breaking my heart," said the kindly Mrs. Dee. "I suppose you had to go a roundabout way to mail that letter."

Jack smiled. So did Mrs. Dee.

"There was no letter," said Jack.

"As if you needed to tell me that."

"See you at lunch, Mrs. Dee," said Jack.

"You'll sit down and have some breakfast," said Mrs. Dee. "And you, too, Mr. Macdonald. You both look a little pale to me this morning; especially you, my young storyteller."

There was nothing wrong with Torb, but Jack was nursing a bug in his chest.

"Only one glass of milk. Only one buttered roll. And you've left half your eggs on the plate," said Mrs. Dee. "Why, it didn't pay me to open the kitchen again for that! What's wrong with you, young fellow?"

"Something wrong?" asked Torb, as they moved to their first class of the day.

"Nothing I can't lick," said Jack. "I'll see you at the pool this afternoon if you can make it."

"I'll make it," said Torb.

He wasn't so sure about Jack.

Neither was swim coach Hal Ulen.

"Get that arm back faster! Keep that rhythm!"

Jack was up and out of the water.

"You look beat to me!" snapped Ulen. "You can't stay up

all night and expect to come in here and swim against Yale!"

"I wasn't up all night," Jack thought. "And I'm going to be in there, swimming against Yale!"

He said nothing.

They were lining up for pictures. There was always some photographer around the place.

Jack walked off and joined his brother Joe, who was sitting at the edge of the pool.

"Afraid of breaking the camera?" kidded Joe.

"Let them get a picture of the team," said Jack. "They're always wanting pictures of Joe Kennedy's boys!"

"What's up?" asked Joe Jr.

"Nothing."

"You looked pretty good to me out there," said Joe.

"Coach was right," said Jack. "My arms aren't coming down right. My rhythm's off. I've got to work on it."

"Sure," said Joe. "See you for dinner?"

The two brothers generally had dinner together, or lunch, one meal a day, anyway, though they still had their differences.

Joe was still the big man, and Jack still resisted the authority he pulled on him every now and then. But they were older now. The two years' difference in their ages didn't matter as much as it used to. They had drawn closer to each other.

"I'll be there," said Jack.

But he wasn't.

He stayed in the pool all afternoon, working on his backstroke, working on his rhythm. He had to make the first big Crimson squad against Yale.

It was Torb who pulled him out of the water.

"You need some calories, boy! You've got to have something to burn up with that stroke!"

"You go ahead and eat," said Jack. "I'm not hungry."

"Hungry or not," countered Torb, "you're getting out of that water."

Whatever energy he had started with, it was gone by now. Torb helped him out of the tank.

"You're sick, fellow," he said.

"I'm all right."

"You've got a fever," said Torb. "Get dressed. I'm taking you to the infirmary."

"I'm all right, I tell you," protested Jack.

His legs were weak, his tongue was parched, and he could feel his body burning up with a fever.

74

"Infirmary!" insisted Torb, helping Jack with his sweater. Jack was too weak to protest.

"You've got flu," said the doctor. "There's an awful lot of it around this year."

There was always something, it seemed to Jack, but he was actually relieved. It wasn't jaundice again.

"We'll keep you in bed. You'll be as good as new in about a week," said the doctor.

"A week!" protested the suddenly horrified Jack.

"It'll take all of that and maybe more," said the doctor.

"But the tryouts for the Yale meet are only a week off," Jack said urgently.

"You can forget about the meet," said the doctor.

"No, sir!"

The doctor shrugged his shoulders.

"Even if you're out in a week, you won't have the energy to pull your own weight for ten days and more," he said.

Jack was stunned.

"Nurse," said the doctor, "get this young man to bed."

The fever subsided quickly, but the doctor kept him in bed.

"They can't do this to me," said Jack.

"They seem to be doing it all right," said Torb, sitting at the edge of his friend's bed.

"I'm going to make that Yale meet if it kills me."

"It might do just that," said Torb.

But Jack maneuvered Torb into sneaking a steak into his infirmary room every afternoon.

"Tastes good," said Jack, digging into it hungrily. "I'll need all the energy I can get."

"You're the doctor," said Torb.

"Now get me my robe," ordered Jack.

The orders were followed.

"Now let's get down to the pool!"

"What are you talking about?" Torb Macdonald laughed. It wasn't a laughing matter.

"Nobody is in the pool at this time," said Jack. "I'm going to practice that backstroke and you're going to coach me! I've got to swim in that meet against Yale. It's the biggest race of the year. I want to go against the Bulldog!"

The second afternoon, Torb carried a stop watch.

"How is my time?" asked Jack.

"Not bad," said Torb, wondering himself at Jack's courage and determination. "Don't you think you've done enough?"

"Once more across the pool and back!"

Once more, and once again, when he should have been lying in his infirmary bed, recuperating, regaining his strength, Jack Kennedy was swimming the pool, once more and once again.

He wasn't nearly at his full strength the afternoon of the tryouts for the squad to meet with Yale; yet he won the first heat, the second heat, the third heat. In the fourth heat, he swam against Richard Tregaskis, the man who was to win his way in the world of letters with his *Guadalcanal Diary*.

Neither man, of course, had his mind on anything further in the future than the Harvard-Yale swim meet the next afternoon.

"On your mark! Set! Go!"

The shallow dive, and the race was on.

"Go it, Jack!"

"Go it, Dick!"

Head and head, their arms lifting and coming back to cut the water, their feet churning up the pool rhythmically, magnificently, the two swimmers vied against each other for the coveted spot in the Yale meet.

"Come on, Dick!"

"Come on, Jack!"

The big letter H was the prize to the winner. The two Crimson men gave it all they had.

It was Tregaskis who began to forge ahead.

"Go it, Jack!"

But his arms grew heavy. His breath began to come too quickly. The flu had taken its toll. Jack lost ground. He was not nearly so strong as he had hoped to be, as he had imagined he was.

"Good luck," he said to Dick Tregaskis, shaking his hand warmly, but he could not conceal his own disappointment. Not only was he out as lead man in the backstroke; he was completely out of the meet.

"I don't think I can get back into shape quickly enough," he wrote home to his mother. "It means a whole season has gone to waste."

But college isn't all athletics. It is history and literature and government and art and mathematics and the sciences. Jack wasn't the best of students in his freshman and sophomore years at Harvard; at least, his grades were not among the best. Nor did he participate in the political activites that were rampant in the Harvard Yard in those turbulent days of the late thirties. Hitler was moving rapidly toward his blitzkriegs. Spain was torn by civil war. Japan was waving its long swords and its more modern machines of battle. A young man brought up in the tradition of state politics, whose father was a national political figure, could not possibly avoid the issues that had both hemispheres, east and west, on tenterhooks. Jack avoided the undergraduate activities, which included parading, picketing, organizing into clubs of one kind or another, but he was fully aware of what was going on in the trouble zones of Europe and Asia, that at any moment the whole world might become embroiled in a struggle for survival.

He got in touch with Les Billings. Les was still at Princeton.

"Let's see something of Europe before it all blows up," he said.

Les was still going it on a very limited income. "I can manage it," he said, "but we'll have to stay clear of first-class hotels and that kind of stuff."

They went by boat in the least expensive way. It was to be a pleasure trip, and that's the way it started. Shuffleboard, deck tennis, dancing at night, the captain's dinner, they participated in it all and enjoyed it all. It was "Parlez-vous français?" when they landed at Le Havre, but the hard realities of the European situation brought a quick change in the attitudes of the young men and in their approach to their holiday.

"No, we are not worried," said a Frenchman, answering Jack's query. "Let that monster shout all he wants to shout in Berlin. We have the Maginot Line."

The Maginot Line was a series of fortified pillboxes the French had erected along the length of their border with Germany. The boast was that there was no military force strong enough to breach it.

"The Maginot Line will hold them," said the Frenchman, speaking of the growing Nazi horde.

History was going to prove him wrong, the whole French nation wrong, in only a few brief years, but Jack, too, found some comfort in the certainty, however mistaken it was, of the French citizenry.

In Paris, they found a small room for eighty cents a day. It was about all that Les Billings could afford, and it was good enough for Jack Kennedy. A room is only for sleeping. The days were spent roaming the crooked little streets of the Left Bank, the crooked little streets of the Right Bank, visiting the Louvre, the tomb of Napoleon, taking in all the

77

sights and eating on the checkered tablecloths in the side-street cafés and restaurants.

They moved into Italy, climbed Mount Vesuvius, the terrible volcano that had swallowed the thriving city of Pompeii. They moved into Spain and talked with the people involved in the great civil struggle. They saw the bull-fighting in Biarritz and looked in on the gambling tables of Monte Carlo.

They were young; they were eager; they were earnest. The sights were impressive and the newness was exciting; but it was more than the novelty and the scenic splendors of the Old World that left their mark on the boys from Princeton and Harvard. It was the undercurrent of fear in France, for all its brave words, the terrible tales of the Spanish refugees fleeing their war-torn country, the noises of Hitler throughout Europe that opened their eyes to the potential catastrophe so soon to tear up whatever peace was left in the world.

"People in the United States are almost completely ignorant of what is happening in Europe," Jack wrote his father, indicating his growing awareness, his suddenly developing political maturity.

In Italy, he had visited with the Pope's secretary, Cardinal Pacelli, and he had been in audience with the Pope at the Vatican. The prayers for peace in the high seat of the Roman Catholic Church were comforting to the soul, but there, too, the imminence of the great bloody struggle was too much apparent.

Jack Kennedy returned to Harvard in the fall of 1937 a more serious young man, a more serious young student. He knew Europe would sooner or later burst into flame. He knew, too, that once Europe was embroiled, the United States could not keep away from the fires across the Atlantic.

11

Jack spoke vigorously but thoughtfully. Professor Arthur Holcombe, chairman of the Government Department at Harvard, listened patiently and respectfully.

"I'm going to do my thesis on Bertrand Snell," said Jack, "if that is satisfactory with you, sir."

"Can you tell me a little more about it?" asked the professor. "Why Snell? And just precisely what are your intentions with this paper?"

Professor Holcombe was pleased enough with this sudden sign of serious effort on the part of the Harvard sophomore. He was probing now for a stronger committal and a more assured purpose.

"Bertrand Snell is not particularly well known," said Jack. "He's a rather obscure leader in New York politics. Besides, he is a Republican."

"Yes?" Professor Holcombe waited.

"It will require more research than I imagine you require ordinarily," went on Jack.

"That's true," agreed his mentor.

"He is a Republican, as I said before," continued Jack. "You suggested I broaden the base of my understanding. I haven't had much to do with Republicans before."

He smiled. So did the professor.

"I've been surrounded by Democrats all my life," said Jack. "I guess Bertrand Snell isn't going to corrupt me."

"No," commented Professor Holcombe. "I don't think corruption lies anywhere in honest research, and if it means anything to you, I'm glad for your choice and I approve completely of your approach. I expect a fine thesis."

He got it.

Football, swimming, sailing were still to occupy Jack Kennedy. The Kennedys would always be occupied with one sport and another. But time had begun to move Jack, though he was not yet aware of it, to the ultimate career and goal of his life. His turn to serious study was the beginning.

In the late fall of that year, his father, Joseph Kennedy,

who had filled two important posts for Franklin Delano Roosevelt, was appointed to his third and most important position in the Roosevelt administration. The grandson of an Irish immigrant, the son of a man who had moved himself from saloonkeeper to political eminence in the city of Boston, he was named by the President of the United States as America's Ambassador to the Court of St. James's in London.

Boston was elated. The American Irish, all over the forty-eight states, did a jig in celebration.

"Now what is an Irishman doing in the Court of St. James's?"

"What is a Catholic, with the Pope's blessing on him, doing in a Protestant palace?"

"He's a Knight of Malta and a Grand Knight of the Order of Pius IX. Will he be bowing to a British sovereign?"

"Does an Irishman, even if he is an American Irishman, bow down to any king of England?"

It was all tongue-in-cheek of course. Joseph Kennedy was first and always an American. He was to represent the people of the United States, Catholic, Protestant, Jewish, or of any other faith. He was to represent the country. With five of their nine children, Joe Kennedy and his wife, Rose, moved across the sea.

Joe Jr. and Jack, of course, remained at Harvard. Rosemary stayed on at Marymount Convent in Tarrytown, New York, and Eunice continued at the Sacred Heart Convent in Noroton, Connecticut.

"They'll visit with us in the summer and whenever else they can," said Rose Kennedy, still the gray-eyed, dark-haired beauty, "but I wouldn't think of interrupting their schooling."

Education was always the number one activity for the Kennedy children, as Rose saw it. She was interested in the athletic achievements of her sons and daughters, but learning was most important. Dad Kennedy got the news from the football field, the swimming meets, the sailboat competitions; Rose Kennedy wanted to know how they were doing in their studies. Jack satisfied them both throughout his years at Harvard. He was never a star athlete, though he tried and never gave up, and this was pleasing to Joe Sr. It was his maturing and his growing interest and work in the areas of government and foreign affairs that pleased both his mother and father.

"Torb is out for two weeks, but we hope he can play in the Penn game this Saturday," he wrote his father.

But he also wrote, in the same letter, "I gave an hour talk to the YWCA and the YMCA."

Studies and sports were claiming him more fiercely. One afternoon, on the football field, the game claimed him too fiercely.

Two elevens, in practice, playing the ball as if their letters depended on it, crashed head-on. There was a huge tangle of arms and legs on the scrimmage line. Slowly, one player after another extricated himself from the mass. One player, however, got up more slowly than the rest.

"Trouble?" asked Torb Macdonald, who had been watching the Junior Varsity practice session.

"It's all right," said Jack, but he was obviously in pain.

"Get over to the bench," said Torb.

"All right, Coach," kidded Jack, "after the game."

"Now!" said Torb.

He signaled the bench.

"Why did you do that?" protested Jack.

But the coach called him in.

"Your back?"

"Just a strain."

"You'd better sit it out," said the coach.

Jack sat it out. He sat on the bench for a long time. His injury was more serious than he realized. It was to get worse. In years to come it was nearly to cost him his life.

But young Kennedy wasn't paying much attention to injuries just then, and if he wasn't running interference, blocking, or grabbing the forward pass on the gridiron, he was on the swimming team, backstroking for Harvard, or sailing for its Varsity crew. Actually, it was in the water that Jack Kennedy was at his best in collegiate competition.

In June, Harvard sent its sailing crews to Wianno, Massachusetts, to race against Yale, Dartmouth, Princeton, Cornell, Brown, Penn, M.I.T., and Williams. The stake was the MacMillan Cup and the collegiate championship, and Joe Kennedy, Ambassador to the Court of St. James's in London, made a special trip to watch his sons participate in the great races.

The teams were well matched, the scoring, at first, close, but Williams, surprisingly, began to pull away. Only Harvard seriously threatened the Williams bid for the coveted cup, and the Crimson was a full five points behind the leader.

Both Joe Jr. and Jack were in the Harvard boat for the last race of the meet. Jim Batchelder, Don Reed, Dick Burnett, Jim Rousmaniere, and Edward Hutton were there with them.

"We can still win it, fellows!" said Joe Jr.

"Can and will!" said Ed Hutton.

"Let's go!" shouted Jack.

Ambassador Kennedy's eyes were on his boys, and his boys knew it.

"We'll take this for Dad," said Joe.

"That's a promise!" said Jack. "And a Kennedy keeps his promise!"

The wind was sharp. It bellied the sails of the Harvard boat, the Williams boat, the Yale boat, every boat in the race.

The gun, and the sailors moved to their tasks, moved to the goal!

The waters were choppy. It required ·consummate skill to maneuver the tight ships along the given course, to hew close to the given path. Extra yards meant extra time, and time was the essence in the race.

"Come on, Joe!" yelled Jack to his brother, as the boat veered sharply around a buoy.

For the Kennedys, it was Hyannisport all over again.

"Keep her going, Jack!" yelled Joe.

The boats, with the emblems of their colleges flying in the wind, kept close, bow and stern with each other. The big sails in the big wind were beautifully white against the blue-green waters.

"Keep her moving, Dick!"

"That's the way, Joe!"

Slowly the Crimson banner moved to the front.

"Take it!" yelled Joe, as the boat snaked about another buoy in the course.

"Harvard!"

"Williams!"

"Princeton!"

"Yale!"

They could hear the shouting from the shore now, but they had no time to turn their faces to it.

They were nearing the finishing line. The shouting grew louder, sharper, more pressing.

Harvard kept its lead, increased its lead.

"Harvard!"

"Harvard!"

It was Harvard, its Crimson banner high, that streaked across the last mark first, and it was Harvard that came from five points behind to win the MacMillan Cup, the intercollegiate sailing championship.

"You did it!" said Joe Kennedy, Sr., shaking the hand of his namesake heartily.

"You did it!" he said, grasping the hand of smiling Jack.

"We Kennedys don't come in second!" he said.

Joe Sr. was a proud ambassador, a proud father. His sons gave him many reasons to be proud. They would give him more, as the years rolled by. And Joe Sr. would always be there, helping his boys to accomplish those deeds, those feats that were to make him the proudest of all fathers in America.

"I suppose you're expecting a nice long vacation after this," he said to Jack, when the boys were dressed and drinking milk and eating chocolate pie after a good healthy dinner. "Not that you haven't earned it," added the Ambassador.

"What's on your mind, Dad?" asked Jack.

He knew a leading question when he heard one.

"I was thinking you might like to mix a little pleasure with a little work this summer," said Joe Sr.

"Sounds all right to me," said Jack, waiting for more to come.

"How would you like to work around the embassy this summer?" asked the Ambassador, finally coming to the point.

"At the Court of St. James's?"

"In London," said Joe Sr.

"As an attaché or something like that?" asked Jack.

"Not quite," said his father. "But you might enjoy working around the office. I was thinking you might learn something about the diplomatic service. You might even like it. You might want to make a career of it."

"I might," said Jack.

"It's not going to be a holiday for you, Jack," said his mother, Rose, when she was consulted. "Dad has a definite plan of work arranged for you. It won't be easy. Dad always believes in hard work for any kind of results worth talking about. You won't just be sitting around to collect your salary. And that, I mean the salary, isn't going to be too much, either."

Actually, Jack did more than office work when he assumed the task his father had set. He worked more as a confidential aide to the Ambassador. He moved around Europe, from country to country, observed, talked with people high and low, observed some more; then he reported to his father on his observations. It was great training. It was great experience. It would all stand him in good stead later on in his young life.

Jack took Torb Macdonald with him on this venture. Torb didn't take six months' leave from Harvard in his junior year, as Jack had to, for the sake of the job; but he was in Europe with the Harvard track team at the time.

Torb couldn't think of a better thing to do. It was good experience, good training, for him, too.

Hitler had already won his mighty victory over the rest of Europe with his triumph at Munich. The Führer's might had swallowed Czechoslovakia. He ranted violently into his microphones, reviewed the vast hordes of goose-stepping German soldiers, their tremendous tanks, their huge air fleet, and violently abused his neighbors with threats of war and invasion.

The two young men ventured into some of the most troubled spots on the continent.

They spent several weeks in Paris. Ambassador William Bullitt was their host, but they walked the streets and talked to the people. They went to Poland, next on the list of Adolf Hitler's proposed victims. They toured through Latvia and the Baltic regions. They visited in Russia, Palestine, then under British rule, traveled through the Balkans, Budapest, Danzig. They trekked through Italy and into Germany. In Berlin, mistaken for Englishmen, they were subjected to a barrage of stones thrown by Nazi hoodlums.

"We're not British," said Jack, "but nothing excuses this kind of bullying tactic!"

He reported dutifully to his father on everything he saw and heard. He offered, too, his analyses of the situations as he saw them, and his opinions were sharp, to the point, and weighted with clear logic.

"The Polish people will not give up Danzig to Hitler, not without fighting for it," he wrote.

"The German people are being whipped into a fierce hatred for the British."

He was an eyewitness to it. He had paid for it as well.

The situation in Palestine was more complicated, but the young Kennedy analyzed it well.

"Britain's policy is sound; it is just and fair, but that isn't enough. They need a policy that will work."

Most important was his conclusion that war was imminent, that Adolf Hitler was on the verge of sending all Europe into flames.

He was correct.

Before the summer of 1939 was over, the holocaust was to break loose and the whole world turned into a field of bloody battle.

"What part do we play in this?" Jack asked his father. "What will be the position of the United States?"

"I'm the Ambassador to England, son," answered Joseph Kennedy, Sr. "I'm not the Government."

"We couldn't stay out of the last one," pursued Jack, referring to World War I and the entry of the United States into the battle against Germany on the side of Great Britain and France and their allies. "Can we expect to stay out of the one that is coming? Do we have a right to stay out of it?"

Jack had begun to admire the English. He had begun to respect their attitudes, their diplomacy, their courage against odds.

"There's no war yet," said Joseph Kennedy, Sr. "Don't you think it's a little too early to be making the kind of decision you're asking about?"

"After what I've seen, Dad," said Jack, "and after what I've heard, I don't think there is too much time left to us for making decisions. It's right on us, Dad, and breathing hot, like the wind. More like a tornado."

"Sometimes the wheels of diplomacy turn slowly, Jack," cautioned his father. "There are still a number of possibilities, alternatives to war. Let's work on those first. Europe has been at peace for only twenty-one years, and that's just a relative peace. It still remembers too well all the scars of the last war. I think there will be much thinking, much effort, to avoid another."

Joe Kennedy, Sr., wasn't mistaken in his knowledge of the feelings in Europe. People wanted almost anything but guns and battle. He hoped, too, as most of Europe hoped, that war could be avoided. But there were forces abroad that Joe Kennedy could not control. It was going to cost him dearly.

It was his own sons, his own daughters, he had in mind when he prayed for peace.

"We can try," he said to his son Jack.

"We can pray," said Jack's mother.

There were prayers. There were prayers throughout he world.

But Adolf Hitler did not pray.

On September 1, 1939, under orders from the Führer, and violating all treaties Germany had signed, the swastika-marked tanks rumbled across the Polish-German frontier, shooting and killing. Swastika-marked planes filled the air, swept across Polish skies, dropped their heaviest bombs, destroying, killing. Soldiers in gray, the swastika fixed on their uniforms, motorcycled, trucked, marched into Poland, shooting, killing. Without any warning, without any word, without a declaration of war, the Nazi hordes plunged the world again into the nightmare of battle and sudden death.

Britain and France were by treaty bound to the defense of Poland. Britain and France hold their word sacred. On September 3, 1939, totally unprepared for the kind of warfare Hitler had unleashed, inadequately prepared for any kind of war, both Britain and France, by honor bound, declared that a state of war existed between Hitler's Third Reich and their countries of England and the Republic of France.

"What now, Dad?" asked Jack.

The answer came, though it was only a partial answer, a prelude of what was to follow, on the night of September 3, only two short and hectic days after the beginning of the frightful Armageddon.

12

The British transatlantic liner, *Athenia*, sailed smoothly through the waters of the North Atlantic. It carried, in addition to its full crew, some fifteen hundred passengers, including somewhat more than three hundred Americans. Its destination was Montreal in Canada. Its destiny was something else.

The outbreak of war in Europe had filled the ship with refugees from the conflict. It had also cut short the vacations and the business trips of American nationals—Canadians and Mexicans, as well as those from the United States. Everyone was eager to reach the comparative safety of a North American port.

Glasgow, the point of departure, was some two hundred miles away the evening of September 3. There was nothing but water on all horizons to be seen by the passengers who strolled along the decks or lounged comfortably in their deck chairs. Down below, mothers and fathers were putting their children to sleep or getting ready for bed themselves. The crew, of course, tended to its business of keeping the ship moving.

"A beautiful night."

"Too bad we had to cut this trip short."

"Dinner was good."

"Steward, do you think you can find me an extra blanket?"

Except for the undercurrent of tension, which the outbreak of war inevitably brings, the *Athenia's* voyage, with a full complement of passengers, seemed routine. There was little talk of war. There was less talk of any possible danger.

"Unrestricted submarine warfare is a thing of the past," declared one tourist.

"Imagine striking a ship without warning!" declared a young lady who found it difficult to conceal her nervousness. "It's barbaric!"

"That was in the last war," said a young fellow passenger, comfortingly. "You don't have to worry about anything like that. It can't happen to us."

"No," added a third passenger. "They've all signed some

kind of treaty on it. Germany, too. They have to get us off the ship before they sink it."

The young lady cast her eyes on the deep black waters of the cold Atlantic.

"That's a great help," she said.

Seventy-five per cent of the passengers were women and children. There were about a hundred college girls, mostly from the University of Texas, aboard the liner.

"The way Hitler has been tearing up one treaty after another," said an older man, quietly, as if he were not too sure that he wanted to be heard, "I'm afraid anything might happen."

The engineers checked the six steam turbines of the ship. The officer on watch scanned the waters for any possible sign of trouble. Sparks checked his radio equipment. The master of the ship was constantly on the phones, checking the engine room, checking radio, checking the officer on watch.

In the darkness of the night, completely submerged in the waters, except for its conning tower, a Nazi U-boat trailed its prey.

Eight hundred yards from the steamer, the submarine and its murderous Nazi crew raised the conning tower, took careful aim, and discharged a deadly torpedo into the side of the unsuspecting liner.

There was smell of cordite, the loud blast of an explosion. "We've been hit!"

The officer on watch sounded the alarm—eight short blasts and one long one—on the ship's siren.

He saw the conning tower now! He saw the submarine submerge and disappear!

Eight short blasts! One long one!

The deck was alive with men and women and children racing for the lifeboats.

"I was down below," said Tom Connely of New York later, "with my wife and my three sons, Francis who is nine years old, Raymond eight, and Tom three. We were all in our stateroom, but only Tom was in bed when, without warning, the explosion occurred. We didn't have to be told what had happened. We knew.

"We threw some clothes on the child and made a dash for the lifeboats. One of the hatches had blown right up through the deck. Many passengers were badly injured by the flying splinters. My wife had a deep gash in her forehead. It was bleeding profusely. But we had no time to attend to it. Our main concern was to get into the safety of the lifeboats.

"The ship's officers helped. They kept our family together. Of course we had nothing salvaged but the clothes we were wearing. We are grateful for the kindness and the concern that was shown us."

Others were not so fortunate.

Mrs. Fisher of New York looked for her son among the survivors.

"He's sixteen years old," she said.

She kept looking from group to group hopefully but in vain.

"I rushed out of my cabin," she said, "when we were struck. I called to my son. I saw him on one of the companionways. I called to him again."

She broke into a sob.

"Before I could reach him," she continued, "everything was plunged into darkness. I have not seen him again."

ATHENIA TORPEDOED. 310 AMERICANS ABOARD.

It was in the middle of the night that the news was flashed to Joseph P. Kennedy, America's ambassador to Great Britain. There was little sleep for members of embassies, ambassadors, diplomats of any rank, in those first days of World War II; nor would there be much time for sleeping during the next five or six years for men and women who represented their nationals abroad. He hadn't had time to close his eyes that fateful night of September 3, 1939, before he was wakened by the urgent call.

"The *Athenia* has been torpedoed, sir."

"Where?"

"About two hundred miles west of the Hebrides."

"Dreadful!"

"Over three hundred Americans on board, sir, according to the report."

It was a British transatlantic liner that had been sunk by an enemy submarine. That was not the direct concern of the Ambassador, however he might have felt about the horror of it. It was the Americans aboard with whom he was concerned.

"Didn't they know the *Athenia* carried American citizens?" he demanded of his informant.

It was a rhetorical question.

"That madman!" he said of Hitler. "There will be no neutrality in this war!"

"Rescue ships are already at the scene," continued the message to the Ambassador.

"Good!" said Kennedy. "And the survivors? How many are there? Where are they being brought?"

"There's no count yet on the survivors, sir. They are being brought to Clyde and Glasgow."

"I'll attend to it," said the Ambassador. "Thank you."

He put on his robe and knocked quietly at Jack's room. He didn't want to disturb the rest of the family. They would hear soon enough.

"I want you dressed and up to Glasgow as fast as you can," said the senior Kennedy to his son. "The *Athenia* with some three hundred Americans on board has been torpedoed."

"Any details, Dad?"

"No more than I've given out. A terrible thing. Get all the details you can from the passengers, the American passengers. This is our duty, our obligation. And see to it that they get some clothes to wear, medical attention, if they need it, food and shelter, of course. And keep your wits about you; this is a trying job."

"And passage home?"

"And passage home."

Jack had been dressing all the while they had been talking.

"I'll keep you informed," he said.

"They've taken a terrific beating," cautioned Kennedy Sr. "It isn't an easy job I'm giving you."

"It's a job I want to do, Dad."

"Of course. I'll speak to Mother in the morning."

Jack was at the door. He hesitated, turned around.

"Does this mean that the United States will become involved in this war against Germany?" he asked.

"I can't say."

"The sinking of the *Lusitania* carried us into the last war," said Jack.

He had already seen enough in his travels through Europe to know the intention of the Führer and his Third Reich. He was already convinced that the United States must sooner or later join the forces against the ambitions of Hitler.

"Will it take us more than a *Lusitania* this time?" he asked.

"We're here to take care of Americans on British soil, Jack," said his deeply troubled father. "We are representatives of the Government of the United States, not the Government."

"Yes, sir."

"Do your job. And keep me informed."

Glasgow was tense with the news of the terrible tragedy. Emotions, held tight, sometimes broke loose. There was anger. There was shouting. There was weeping, too.

Young Jack Kennedy spoke to the ship's men. He spoke to the passengers. Mostly, he listened.

"There was no panic aboard," he was told.

"The passengers moved to the lifeboats in an orderly fashion, women and children first."

John Sorbis, a steward, spoke:

"I was serving dinner when the liner was struck. I took the ten people at my table to their boat stations."

John McEwan, the second mate, said: "When my chum and I heard the explosion, we went to our boat stations through the smoke which followed the explosion. We saw the submarine come to the surface, and to our amazement and horror we saw her turn a gun upon us and fire two shells."

Glasgow doctors and nurses hurried from survivor to survivor, checking the minor wounds, checking the major wounds, dressing them, redressing them, tending to people in shock. A large number of women sat with their children in their arms, covered with blankets they had hurriedly snatched out of their cabins as they made their way to safety out of the sinking ship.

Jack stopped a boy of about twelve.

"Where did you get that outfit?" he asked.

The boy was wearing white navy ducks several sizes too large for him, but he had been walking about in the jauntiest manner, as if he had just come through the toughest race in the school and had won it.

"A sailor gave it to me!" he announced proudly. "They look good, too," he said.

"They look fine to me," said young Jack Kennedy, glad to find someone who had come through the terrible ordeal with his colors flying high.

There were others, not quite so proud, not quite so jubilant, but grateful and thankful.

"I handed my two-year-old David into a lifeboat that was just about to descend into the water," said Mrs. Kathleen Somerville. "I had to get into another boat myself, but I wanted to make sure my little boy would be saved."

"Of course," said Jack, a lump in his throat as he watched the mother kiss the head of her sleeping child.

"I was lucky to find another boat," she continued. "Then there were twelve hours in the water, waiting to be picked up. I didn't know for twelve hours whether I would ever see my David again."

"An ordeal," said Jack, knowing there was no word to express the anguish of such a wait as this young mother had experienced.

"But I have him," she said.

And she smiled and kissed her boy again.

There were the less fortunate.

Roy Barrington, all of nine years old, stared into space and wept.

"Where is my mother?" he asked. "Where is my mother?"

No one could tell him.

"Where is my mother?"

Young Jack Kennedy had seen the threat of war in Germany, in Poland, in Italy, in France. This was his first contact with war, with its cruelty, with its inhumanity. This was his first contact with what war does to the ordinary human being, man, woman, child, and infant. The experience burned deeply into his consciousness. There was no time in Glasgow, among the ruins of people's lives, to evaluate it. He had a job on his hands.

He wired what he had seen and heard to his father. His father relayed the message to Washington.

"All on *Athenia* rescued except those killed by the explosion. Admiralty advises me survivors picked up by other ships. Thank God."

Twelve American lives had been lost. Many more Americans had been injured, a number severely.

Jack Kennedy moved from one group to another. There were people to comfort, the wounded to be cared for—hospitalization, doctors, nurses. There was the clamor among the survivors, both injured and whole, to get home, to get back to their own country, to get back to the United States.

"The Ward Steamship Company is sending the *Orizaba*," said Jack.

"We want a convoy," said the passengers who had been rescued from the *Athenia*.

"The *Orizaba* will pick you up and take you to New York," said Jack Kennedy.

"We want a convoy!" demanded the Americans who had come through one ordeal on the Atlantic and who were understandably worried about another.

"You will be carried to New York in perfect safety," said Jack, not really as sure as he tried to sound.

"We don't want a passenger liner," said the survivors.

"We want a ship with guns."

"We want to be able to destroy the Nazis!"

"We want a convoy!"

Jack was patient. There was no other course. He, too, would have preferred a convoy, but he couldn't say it.

"The Germans won't dare sink an American ship," he said. He wasn't sure.

"They won't want to drive us into the war against them," he said. He wasn't sure of that, either.

"We spent six billion dollars on our Navy," said one survivor who knew his figures. "Why can't we have that convoy?"

"You can't trust the Nazis!" came another angry voice.

"They would just as soon destroy us all," came a third.

Jack wanted to say, "You're right" to each of them, but he knew that it couldn't be done.

"The *Orizaba* will pick you up and deliver you safely on American soil," he repeated.

This was the best he could do. The day of the American convoys was not far off, but on that unforgettable day in Glasgow, the *Orizaba* was all Jack Kennedy could offer.

He reported by wire to his father. He spoke with him on the telephone. His views on the situation were duly recorded, his statements on the *Orizaba* and the impossibility of a convoy at that particular moment in history verified. In London, he conferred with his father again.

"How long, Dad," he asked, "before we become committed to this war?"

His father shook his head.

"England is not prepared," said Jack.

"It will fight," said the Ambassador.

"I'm sure of it," said Jack. "So will France. So will Poland. They can resist. They cannot attack."

Jack Kennedy was only twenty-two years old, a very young man in terms of diplomatic understanding. In September, 1939, however, he knew the score.

It would not be long before his unspoken prophecy became a fact.

13

"Handsome, tall, thin, and high-strung, with an ingrained habit of cocking his legs over the arms of his chair," wrote John Alden who had come to interview the Ambassador's son, soon after his return to the United States, for the *Boston Globe,* "Jack was having a hard time, after such an exciting seven months, in settling down to the humdrum life of a student. Radios, chairs, laundry and valises were scattered helter-skelter in the three room suite at Winthrop House."

The "hard time" was to correlate his work at Harvard with his mature understanding of a world partially and soon wholly to be submerged in flames.

He would still swim. He would sail. He played hockey with his "house team." He was elected a class officer. He was still all out for the Crimson football team. But the world of politics, diplomacy, war had crashed into Jack's peaceful life at school. He could not, he did not want to forget it.

"The football games have all been thrillers," he wrote to his mother and father in England, "even though Harvard has been taking a licking. Army beat us 20-17 on a last minute forty-yard pass play. Ben Smith, who is rooming with Torb and me, is now playing first string, and he is very good."

But even football takes second place when war is abroad and threatens one's homeland.

Jack registered for the normally required number of courses at the college. He registered for extra courses to make up for his loss of time.

"Kennedy came back from working in his father's office in London (the United States Embassy in Britain) a greatly matured young man," said Professor Holcombe. "His mental powers were much greater, sharper. He was a keen observer. He would not commit himself to a position until he was sure. Then he would always give himself leeway to compromise or modify his position."

There were the usual bull sessions in Winthrop Hall, the usual student arguments with Torb Macdonald and Ben Smith. There was time out for play and time out for a game on the hockey field. But there was serious work ahead, and Jack went at it with a new vitality and a real and reasoned purpose.

"I took the quarterly French exam yesterday," he wrote to his father. "It was on the work that they had done this year, and they just decided Saturday to make me take it. So I'm very worried about my French mark."

For the first time in all his schooling, his classes became of utmost importance to him. He was no longer satisfied with the so-called "Gentleman's C." He became a B student and an A student.

"This business of making up work is still going on and has to be finished before Thanksgiving. Have made up most of it, but it is hard work to get it very solidly and still do the daily work. Took my first liver injection today, and hope they work. Was wondering what my allowance would be? Could you let me know, as I want to arrange my budget. Will it be the same as Joe's last year? Love, Jack," he wrote to his father in London.

He was eager to make up for lost time. He was earnest about it.

"He'll do it well enough," said his mother, and she was quite happy for the turn of events in Jack's approach to his college requirements. Learning was still the basic and fundamental basis for maturing, according to Rose Kennedy.

To his father, Jack wrote, "Things have been going very well here. I imagine they are keeping you plenty busy. I am enclosing an editorial I had written in the Crimson. The editorial chairman changed it a bit and didn't emphasize some of the things I wanted him to, but nevertheless I think the idea was good, although we were the only ones to advocate it, and though there were quite a few opponents to it. Joe spoke very well last night over "We, the people," and got a big hand. Walter Winchell gave his article in the Atlantic Monthly a big boost last night on his radio program."

Jack Kennedy was beginning to participate for the first time in the life of the whole student body at Harvard, but it was not on a school level; it was with the understanding of the forces abroad in the world and the need to tackle them.

"Everyone here is still ready to fight till the last Englishman, but most people have a fatalist attitude about America getting in before it is over—which is quite dangerous."

The handwriting was on the wall, and Jack Kennedy read it plainly. He was not alone in the fall of 1939 and the spring of 1940, but he was in the minority.

He determined to get at the roots of the evil that had

sprung Hitler loose on the world. The Nazi hordes had already swept through Poland; their planes and tanks had blitzed through Denmark, Holland, Norway. The Maginot Line of the French had failed.

"It started with Munich."

This was the popular conception.

The British ministers, Baldwin first, then Chamberlain, and Chamberlain most, were blamed for the surrender of power to the Führer at Munich, where Hitler got Czechoslovakia without firing a shot.

"Can it be one man? Can it be any small group of men?" Jack asked Professor Bruce Hopper.

"That is one school of thought," said the professor.

"I'd like to do some work on it," said Jack. "I'd like to do some digging, some research on it."

"It sounds like an interesting honors paper," commented Professor Hopper.

"I'd like the honors," said Jack. "More important, I'd really like to know. I want to know."

Jack Kennedy began to spend more time in Harvard's Widener Library than he did in Winthrop Hall.

"Where have you been?" asked Torb.

"I found some interesting clippings in the *London Times*, 1936," said Jack.

"It's got you going, hasn't it?" said Torb.

"I think we're all involved in it," answered Kennedy. "Don't wait for me for dinner. I've got a few notes I want to check first."

"All right," said Macdonald. "But I want to see you down at the swimming pool later. All work and no play . . . you know the rest."

Dr. Payson Sibly Wild, professor of International Affairs and an expert in the field, checked on Jack's work in progress.

"You're doing fine," he said. "You're doing fine."

All winter, all spring, Jack worked on his thesis, temporarily titled "Appeasement at Munich."

Meanwhile, Hitler's armies marched.

The paper Kennedy was working on grew, as he discovered new article after new article, as he pored over the minutes of the meetings of the British Parliament, as he checked into report after report on the progress of the Nazi party, the birth of the Third Reich, the breaking of the Versailles Treaty. The paper grew, and its importance grew, and Jack was aware of it. He gave it everything he had.

"Big party tonight, Jack. Pretty girls, too," said Torb.

"Everyone will be there," said Ben Smith.

"Sorry," said Jack. "I've got this work to finish before morning."

"Take another day for it," said Torb.

"You've got a couple of weeks," said Ben.

As often as not, Jack would stay home. When he went, too tired to battle the good will of his roommates, he didn't stay for long.

"I didn't get much sleep last night," he apologized, saying good night.

"We'll be right along," said Torb.

"Don't break it up for me," pleaded Jack. "I've really got to hit the sack."

Sometimes he would leave without saying good night. It was easier that way.

In either case, when Torb and Ben finally got home, there was Jack, working away under the lamp on some small-print clipping, some lengthy report by a member of Parliament; or else he was fast asleep, in his bed, but completely dressed.

"It sure has him," said Ben Smith.

"It's got us all," said Torb.

One night they came in, the two roommates of the Ambassador's son, and Jack frantically called on them to be still.

"Quiet, fellows! Quiet!"

"Hush!" said Torb in mock respect.

"Hush!" said Ben Smith.

They tiptoed to Jack's desk, looked over his shoulder.

"Quiet, fellows. Please!" pleaded Jack.

The two boys shrugged their shoulders, sat down in their chairs, kicked off their shoes, and did what they were told to do.

For a few minutes, there was absolutely no noise in the room except for Jack's quick pen, and then that noise stopped too.

Ben Smith looked to Torb for a signal.

Torb pointed to Jack.

Jack was going to give the signal that night.

It wasn't long in coming.

For another minute, Jack shuffled his papers, read what he had just written, dropped the papers in a heap, then turned around to his roommates.

"Is it all right to talk now?" asked Torb in sign language.

Jack smiled.

"We've got our freedom!" yelled Torb to Ben Smith.

"Yahoo!" yelled Ben, springing to his feet and doing a fancy imitation of an Indian war dance.

"Let me do the dancing," said Jack.

The three of them danced around, and Ben made war whoops as if he were born to them.

"And now tell us why?" asked Torb, stopping abruptly in his tracks.

"It's finished!" announced Jack.

"Finished!" echoed Torb.

"All done," said Jack.

Torb's immediate reaction was to call for a celebration, but the words died in his mouth. This was a serious work; Torb knew how serious and what it meant to Jack.

"Let's see it," he said.

They read page after page that night, and late into the night, throwing one quote after another at each other.

"You've got something, Jack."

"This is great, Jack."

"We'll wait to hear from Dr. Wild and Professor Hopper," said the very tired Mr. Kennedy.

"Finished my thesis," he wrote to his father. "It was only going to run about the average length, 70 pages, but finally ran to 150. Am sending you a copy. It is the third carbon, as the other two had to be handed in. It was finally titled 'Appeasement at Munich: The Inevitable Result of the Slowness of the British Democracy to Change from a Disarmament Policy.' Thanks a lot for your wire. Worked it in. I'll be interested to see what you think of it, as it represents more work than I've ever done in my life."

The burden of his thesis was that Baldwin and Chamberlain were not the real culprits of the Munich Pact, the opening wedge for Hitler's war on Europe. He blamed the notorious pact on the apathy of the peoples of Europe, their smugness in outmoded defenses. He blamed it on the people's concern with profits and on their concern for a false sense of security. He blamed it on the people's unwillingness to face the facts of a threatening danger and on their opposition to rearming to meet it. Munich, he felt and wrote, was the logical result of such feelings, such attitudes, and such lack of proper action.

Dr. Wild and Professor Hopper were impressed, deeply impressed, with the work of their student.

"I think you might have this published," said Professor Hopper.

"It certainly is worth trying," said Dr. Wild.

Ambassador Kennedy hadn't been consulted, but he was of the same opinion.

"I have shown your thesis to various people around here. (In England) Everyone agrees that it is a swell job, and that you must have put in some long hard hours assembling, digesting and documenting all of this material. . . . I suggest that when you are going over the material again, you check your references. I have found several instances where you have misspelled names and got your dates wrong."

Jack checked, rechecked, dates, names, spelling, documents. He sent it out to a publisher.

"Harpers turned down my book," he wrote to his father. "They felt that France's defeat has changed the interest of the book."

Meanwhile, Jack was graduated *cum laude*. He received a *magna cum laude* for his thesis.

"TWO THINGS I ALWAYS KNEW ABOUT YOU," Joe Kennedy, Sr., cabled to his son when he heard the news. "ONE THAT YOU ARE SMART TWO THAT YOU ARE A SWELL GUY LOVE DAD"

Rose Kennedy came from England for the exercises. Joseph Kennedy, Sr., unhappily could not attend. The war was too pressing. He could not leave his post. It was a proud moment for Jack's mother. This was the second of her sons to receive a degree from Harvard.

"Thanks for the wonderful graduation present," wrote Jack to his father. "It was nice of you to think of it and it will enable me to remain solvent. I am heading for Yale Law School. I think it best I continue my education in international law. I know you agree with me. Bill Coleman is going to Virginia Law School. Torb is going to play pro baseball for a New York Yankee farm team. He's getting $2,000 for the summer, so will be able to pay his way through Law School. The Boston club offered him $1,500. He's feeling much better towards sports. Incidentally I got up a Red Cross Drive at school the last three weeks and raised $1,700, which was $500 over the quota."

Graduation was important, the gift from his father was important, he was still interested in sports and in the careers of his friends, but the war was of paramount importance. He had raised $1,700 for the Red Cross.

And his thesis was important. It was more important now, as Hitler prepared to unleash his merciless bombardment of the British Isles.

Jack sent his manuscript to Wilfred Funk, Inc.

They read the book. They liked it.

"We'll publish it," they said. "Give us another title."

Why England Slept was what Jack offered, based on a suggestion made by Arthur Krock of *The New York Times*.

"That's it," said his publisher.

Henry Luce, publisher of *Time*, read the manuscript. He agreed to write an introduction for the book.

The book appeared in the bookshops across the nation.

"Guns versus Butter," was the headline of one review.

"Young Kennedy's Book," was another.

"Kennedy's Son Urges U.S. Avoid Arms Delay," was the news note of the day.

"England as a Warning to Americans."

"Kennedy Hopes U.S. Will Not Sleep as Britain Did."

"A startlingly timely, strenuously objective 252-page book," a reviewer wrote.

"He is also an extraordinarily astute appraiser of governmental policy and social trends," another wrote.

"No apology need be made on the grounds of the author's youth," was another comment.

Prophets in 1940. How soon were such words to be used again, coupled with the name of John Fitzgerald Kennedy?

Just barely twenty-three years old, Jack had fulfilled one of the promises of his boyhood. He had become a writer, and an important writer. Forty thousand copies of *Why England Slept* were sold in America. An equal number of copies were sold in England. The book was a best-seller. More important, Jack Kennedy's was a voice to be heard and considered in the field of political science and political affairs, national and international.

Jack was pleased, as any successful author must be with such immediate success. His mother and father were proud. Churchill was sent a copy of the book. Harold Laski, old ideological antagonist of Joe Kennedy, received it. The Ambassador sent the King of England a copy of his son's book. It was a high moment in the lives of that close-knit Kennedy family. There were to be others, but not immediately. War has a way of interrupting the steady and solid growth of a continent, a country, a city, a family. There were hard and bitter days ahead for the world. There were hard and bitter days ahead for the Kennedys.

14

By the summer of 1940, the armies of Adolf Hitler had taken Luxembourg, invaded the Netherlands and Belgium. The Maginot Line was broken, and the Germans had paraded triumphantly through the Arc de Triomphe in Paris. What remained of the Allied troops, the French and the British, was seemingly hopelessly pocketed against the English Channel and was rescued only by the almost miraculous action of the British Navy and individual Britons at Dunkirk. The Führer was already claiming victory over England. The terrible and heroic air Battle of Britain had begun, the Nazi planes hurling their deadly bombs, their blockbusters, into the hearts of many cities and towns in that brave little island.

In the United States, the Selective Service System had been inaugurated.

For the first time in our history, the United States, still at peace technically and diplomatically, was drafting men and recruiting women into its largest army, its largest navy, its mightiest air force. Joe Sr.'s service as ambassador to England was over.

"We're getting into it fast," said Joe Kennedy, Jr.

The Kennedys were at their dinner table. It had been a long, beautiful day of swimming, sailing, and golfing in their Hyannisport summer home. But, as usual, there was little of trivial talk among them. The matter under discussion was the war, as it was in almost every American home that summer and would be for many summers to come.

"We're in an awful hurry to start shooting," said Joe.

"It's inevitable," said Jack.

"That's what you wrote in your book."

"I'd write it again. It needs to be written again and said again."

"That doesn't make it right morally, politically, or any other way," argued Joe Jr. "Build our strength at home, I say. Let Europe take care of itself."

"Would you stop our convoys?" asked Eunice.

"Of course! Send a convoy and you're asking for an attack. It's not passengers we're convoying to England; it's arms and munitions and weapons of war. The Germans know it, and they're not going to stand by and just watch."

"They'll attack," said young Bobby Kennedy.

"Of course they'll attack," insisted Joe Jr. "And just let them sink one of our boats and the country is at war!"

"Where we belong," said Jack Kennedy. "This is not Europe's war. It's a world war. We're involved, whether we wish it or not. I say let the involvement be plain, and no mistake about it."

"That means that both of you would be wearing uniforms," said Patricia.

"That's what it means," confirmed Jack. "Perhaps the sooner we wear them, the better."

Rose Kennedy and Joe Kennedy, Sr., listened. Occasionally, they put in a word for Jack; more often it was Joseph Kennedy, Sr., putting in a word for his son Joe.

It was not a simple debate. These were not simply opinions of passion. There was experience; there was thought in every word spoken.

"We should profit from the lesson of the failure of Britain to prepare for this holocaust," said Jack. "We don't have to wait for the Nazi bombs."

It was a debate in which the whole of America was involved. The richest, the poorest, the mill workers, the shipbuilders, the lawyers, the doctors, the teachers, people in every walk of life and in every house, in the streets, the parks, in meeting halls and out, could be heard arguing America's position in the world conflagration, arguing about the part America was playing in it, arguing about the part they wanted America to play.

"Keep us out of it."

"Get into it before it is too late."

"Give them all the help we can, short of war."

"Keep America safe."

"The Nazis must be beaten before they swallow all of Europe."

"If we don't attack Hitler, Hitler will attack us."

The debate was concerned with lives, American lives, the lives of fathers, brothers, sons, daughters. It was an earnest debate, a sincere debate. No word was or could be spoken lightly.

" 'Tomorrow the world,' " said Jack. "These are his words, the words of the Führer. He has a time schedule and we're on that schedule somewhere. I say let's break that schedule. Let's break it now."

Eventually the words would give way to guns and blood and death, and both brothers, Joe and Jack, would be utterly and completely wedded to that struggle. But in the summer of 1940, the two brothers were poles apart in their thinking, in their beliefs. They aired their differences sharply, even bitterly at times, at the dinner table, in the sitting rooms, on the big lawns of Hyannisport, even on and in the waters of Nantucket Sound.

"You're being romantic," Joe Jr. charged.

"I'm being completely realistic," answered Jack.

But for all the hot argument, it was a good summer for the Kennedys, as good as a summer could be in the shadows of the threatening war. For the first time in many years, they were all together again: Joe Kennedy, Sr., Rose, their nine children. They could not know then that it would be the last time all eleven Kennedys would ever be together again. They made the most of it.

"How about sailing the boats?" asked Bobby.

"Race you!" challenged Teddy, who was eight years old now.

"Who's for touch football?" shouted an eager Patricia.

"How about a round of golf, Dad?" asked Joe.

They played, they swam, they sailed, they laughed, and they were together, but try as they might, they could never get too far away from the war in Europe and the struggle of the world for its freedom.

"Tell them about the trouble we had in Madrid," said Kathleen, leaning over to her brother Joe, as the family sat on the lawn in the cool of the early evening.

From February through August, 1939, Joe Jr. had toured all through Spain during its civil war, when the country was torn by shot and shell and, worse, by the hatreds engendered in any war that sets brother against brother. He had been through Loyalist Spain. He had been through Franco-held Spain. Kathleen had been with him in Madrid, the constantly bombarded capital of the unhappy country.

"Tell them about it," said Kick.

"You mean the time I was nearly arrested?"

The Kennedys had heard all the stories Joe brought back, had heard them more than once. They wanted to hear them again.

"No, no," said Kick. "Tell them about the time we went swimming."

"I was nearly arrested then, too," said Joe.

"Why didn't they arrest you?" asked Jack, throwing young Bobby Kennedy a wink.

"Yeah? Why didn't they?" echoed Bobby.

"Because I was too smart," said Joe.

"Tell us about it," ordered young Teddy Kennedy.

"Well," said Kathleen, taking the storyteller's pose, "it was hot that afternoon. It was always hot in Madrid."

"With the bombs exploding all around you," said Eunice.

"Bombs or no bombs, it was hot," said Kick.

"Tell us the story," said Jean Kennedy.

"Well," began Kathleen again, "there wasn't too much by way of bath accommodations. Besides, we preferred to go swimming."

"I'd like to go swimming now," interrupted Jean.

"You will," said Eunice. "Go ahead, Kick."

"Well, we got down to the beach all right, but Joe wasn't wearing the right kind of bathing suit."

"No!" Bobby Kennedy laughed.

"Oh, he was wearing his swimming trunks, pretty much like the swimming trunks he was wearing this afternoon."

"And the police didn't like it?"

"It wasn't the police at first. It was everyone on the beach. They all looked at him, the men and the women and even the kids. They looked at him as if he were some new kind of disease."

"Did he have a rash on his face?" asked Teddy.

"I must have blushed a little," said Joe.

"Why was everyone looking at you?" asked Bobby, as though he had never heard the story before.

"Because everyone else was dressed from his neck down to his ankles, like they did when Grandpa Fitz used to go swimming, and Grandma."

"That must have looked funny!"

"They thought *we* looked funny. Especially Joe!"

"How could they swim in those things?"

"They did, somehow."

"I tried to argue. Did you ever try to argue with a Spanish cop?" asked Joe.

"In your Spanish?" queried Jack.

"I threw in a little French, too," said Joe.

"It didn't help?"

"They're more stubborn than the cops at home. I had to go back to the hotel to get a T-shirt. That made it all right. That made it decent."

"And you got wet?"

"I got wet, but I didn't get much of a sunburn, I tell you."

"That's a funny story," said young Teddy Kennedy, and everybody laughed.

There were other stories Joe had to tell of his journey through Spain. They weren't so funny.

"A British destroyer took me on at Marseilles," he said. "I was suspect the moment I got onto Spanish territory."

"Anybody who would want to walk into a place that was living on gunfire would have to be judged suspect, or mad, or both," said Jack.

"You take your chances if you want to see what's happening on the spot," said Joe.

He had taken his chances. Joe Kennedy, Jr., would always take his chances. He was going to pay for it.

"Have you got your papers?" the vice-consul in the vicinity of Valencia had asked him.

"Sure," said Joe, and he produced two sets of papers.

"Put them away!" shouted the consul.

"What for?" Joe asked. "This is a Franco passport. This is a Loyalist passport."

"Great!" said the consul. "You're in Loyalist territory. Put away that Franco document! Put it away fast!"

Joe shrugged his shoulders and put away the Franco passport.

The consul drew a deep breath. "They're shooting around here first, then asking questions."

"They picked me up anyhow," said Joe. "They were sure I was a spy for somebody or something."

They let him go, of course, and Joe Kennedy, Jr., seemed none the worse for it. As a matter of fact, he seemed to have enjoyed it.

It was Drew Pearson, the Washington journalist, who wrote the story for the press.

"The most that he seems to have done," he wrote of Joe's sojourn among the Loyalists in Madrid, "was to make life miserable for the caretaker of the American Embassy by complaining that he didn't get enough to eat."

"How about it, Joe?" asked Eunice.

"You know there wasn't enough to keep a healthy man well fed," he insisted.

Joe had more trouble with the Franco people. If Madrid thought he was a spy, the Falangists were not to be outdone. They picked him up, as the Loyalists had done. They put him in a cell, as the Loyalists had done. They questioned

105

him, as their antagonists had questioned him. Then they went the Loyalists one better.

"You'll take off all your clothes," they said.

Of course they spoke in Spanish. They also gesticulated, in case Joe didn't understand the language.

Joe demurred. It didn't help.

It was Drew Pearson who broke this story, too, for the press.

"He (Joseph Kennedy, Jr.) was released (by the Falangists) only after his clothes were taken off and lemon juice rubbed on his epidermis to see whether invisible ink messages were written thereon."

"What's epidermis?" asked Teddy Kennedy.

"Skin, Teddy. Skin."

"And were there any messages?" asked Bobby, intrigued by the dark possibilities of the cloak-and-dagger school of intrigue.

"Back and front," kidded Joe.

"Really?" asked the awe-stricken youngster.

"Not even a word, Bobby." Joe laughed, to Bobby's keen and obvious disappointment. "Not even the first letter of a word."

Bobby loved this story best of all the stories Joe Kennedy, Jr., told. He always hoped that at some time it would have a different ending.

Joe had finished his first year at Harvard Law School, and he was already embarked on the political career his father had envisioned for him. He had been named a delegate to the Democratic National Convention, which would nominate the party's candidate for the office of the President of the United States. Here, too, there were going to be differences in the Kennedy family, and this time Jack was going to take the quieter role, while Joseph Kennedy, Sr., would oppose his son in action in the very arena in which he wished Joe to succeed.

The question in 1940 was the third term. No man in our history had been elected to the presidency for three terms. No man had run for three terms.

"George Washington set the precedent. He refused to run for the third term. He saw the danger of monarchy in it."

"There's nothing in the Constitution against a third term, is there?"

"It's an unwritten law. The unwritten law can be, and should be, as strong as the written law."

Young Joe Kennedy went to the Democratic Convention, pledged to vote for James Farley as his party's nominee.

Franklin Delano Roosevelt was nominated for a third term from the floor, despite all the arguments raised against it.

James Farley was nominated from the floor.

Joe Kennedy, Jr., was pledged to Farley. He plumped for Farley.

Joe Kennedy, Sr., went on the air to speak for Franklin Delano Roosevelt.

Joe Kennedy, Jr., stuck with James Farley.

Joe Sr. was approached by Roosevelt partisans.

"You ought to be able to convince your son!"

"We need every vote at the convention!"

"How about it, Joe?"

"My son is quite capable of making up his own mind," answered Joe Kennedy, Sr. "He'll cast his vote the way he sees fit. I'm bringing no pressure on him to ballot any other way than he wants to. I wouldn't think of telling him, or anybody else, how to vote in a party convention."

Jack was with Roosevelt, too, but he wasn't a delegate and he had no power one way or the other. He kept pretty much out of the primary fight, but he believed Franklin Delano Roosevelt was the man best fitted to head the government of the United States through the crucial years.

Joe Kennedy, Jr., cast his ballot for James Farley.

Farley lost. Roosevelt was nominated for a third term in office. He would win that third term, be nominated for a fourth term as President of the United States, and win that, too.

Jack was on the sidelines this time. It was Joe who got his first real taste of political action. There was another kind of action for which he would soon enlist, however, and it was to bring tragedy for the first time into the lives of all the Kennedys.

★ ★
15
★ ★

Jack Kennedy had announced to his family that he was going to enroll in the Yale Law School for the fall of 1940. By mid-summer of that year he was no longer so certain of his choice. His success as an author may have had some influence on his thinking. More likely it was the temper of the times.

"What are the chances of the Republican party in this next election, Dad?"

"Wendell Willkie seems to have a lot of strength."

Willkie had been the surprise nominee of the Republicans at their national convention in Philadelphia. He had come from nowhere to stampede his party into naming him their candidate for the presidency of the United States. He was a dynamic figure. He had dramatic appeal. He had, on his side, the nation's reluctance to break tradition and elect a president to a third term of office in the White House. Perhaps the biggest question everyone was asking was: Which man will steer our country more safely through the troubled waters of a threatening war?

"Do you think Willkie can beat Roosevelt?" asked Jack.

"He might."

The campaigning had started early, and its noise was abroad in every state of the Union. It could not drown out, however, the noise of the battle in the sky, on the land, in the waters of Europe. Nor, for one moment, did it clear the air of the present danger of conflict felt in every home in the United States.

No man's mind was free of the threat of danger in which he lived. No man's mind was at ease.

"How can you make plans for tomorrow when tomorrow everything might explode?" was a question heard on all sides.

Jack had intended to pursue his career at the Yale Law School. He didn't.

"I'm not sure of what I want to do, Dad."

Joe Kennedy, Sr., who still did not think in terms of a political career for Jack, offered a number of possibilities.

"You might travel. You might do a bit of work in foreign

relations. You might even be interested in business. There are a number of good schools that offer good business courses."

Joe Kennedy, Jr., was still his father's hope as far as the political tradition of the Kennedys was concerned.

Jack mulled over the question, the suggestions. There was too much distraction at home, abroad, to allow for certain decision. At the last moment, and not too heartily convinced that he was doing the right thing, he enrolled at Stanford University in California, not for law but for business.

"I'll give it a try," he said.

"It can't hurt," replied his father. "A knowledge of the basic principles of business can prove valuable in any field you might finally go into."

It didn't hurt, and Stanford University had a beautiful campus, but it was neither the course nor the university that Jack wanted. He realized that almost at once, but he had started and he was going to finish whatever he had started, even if it was going to last no more than six months.

September went, October, November, December. Jack began to look through books of maps, through travel guides. He began to think of places he had only heard of or read about. By February, 1941, with the courses he had enrolled in finished, he knew that he was through with school, with all schools, for the time being, anyway.

"I'm on my way to South America," he wrote home. "I'd like to get a better perspective on the other half of our continent."

He packed his bags and he was off. He traveled through Argentina, Brazil, Chile, through the whole of the pear-shaped continent. It was a journey that would stand him in good stead some few years later. In 1941, the trek was only a halfhearted holiday. Even that far from home, the increased tensions of the world could not be lost, the increased tensions of his own country could not be forgotten.

"I'll have to pull some program out of all this," he said to his brother Joe when he got back and saw him at Harvard. "This bouncing around isn't doing me any good, and it isn't getting me anywhere."

"Where do you want to get, Jack? Where do you expect to get?"

"I don't know. That's the whole trouble. How are you doing here in the law school?" asked Jack, trying to find a way out of the doubts that assailed him.

"Not bad," said Joe. "Not bad."

"That's something," said Jack. "At least you know where you're heading."

"That's what it looks like," said Joe solemnly.

"Uh?"

"I'm through after this year," said Joe.

"What are you talking about? You've got another year to go."

"I'll finish this semester, but I'm not going back. Not this September anyway."

"Restless?" asked Jack quizzically.

"No," said Joe. "I'm going to join up."

"Join up what?"

"I'm going to enlist. I'm going to join up with the service."

"Just because you may feel restless," argued Jack, unwilling at the moment to face the facts he knew for facts, "you don't have to jump into uniform! We're all in this together. I know the feeling. It's like wandering around loose in a big house, wanting to get out. There's just one door out, and you know the door, and you just can't get to it to open it."

"I found the door," said Joe.

"I suppose you have," said Jack quietly. The reality of things is sometimes a bit harder to take than things imagined. "But what's your hurry?"

"No hurry," said Joe. "I'm finishing the year at Harvard."

"Then the Army?"

Jack was still fighting the inevitable, not for himself but for his brother.

"The Navy," said Joe. "The Navy Air Corps."

"We'll all be in it sooner or later," Jack said.

"You've been saying that for a long time."

"Why are you going now?" asked Jack.

"The sooner the better. That's what you said, isn't it?"

"I guess so."

"It just hasn't come on me until now," said Joe. "It isn't your speeches that decided me, Jack, even if you'd like to think so."

"No?"

"No," said Joe. "I've been thinking about it for a long time. I had to make up my mind. Now it's made up."

"You've told Dad?"

Joe nodded.

"And Mother?"

"We talked about it," said Joe.

"She isn't very happy about it, I bet," said Jack.

"Come off it, Jack."

"Well, she didn't do a dance about it, did she?"

"And I didn't do a dance either! What's on your mind, Jack? You're not doing a turnabout, are you?"

"No!"

"Then stop making a game of it. You've talked enough about our getting into this thing, stopping Hitler, keeping America, keeping the world free. Have you changed your mind?"

"I'm not trying to stop you, Joe, if that's what you're thinking."

"I don't think you would. You couldn't anyway. For once, I think you were right. I know you were right!"

"Thanks," said Jack.

For a moment there was a dead silence between them. It was like old times, when the two brothers battled away at each other over a sailboat, over a piece of chocolate pie smothered in whipped cream, except that the stakes were somewhat bigger this time and their anger was not with each other but with the state of the world. Like old times, there was the pent-up emotion and the temporary antagonism. Like old times, after the moment, there was the slow grin, then the burst of laughter.

"So I was right for once," said Jack.

"You can't always be wrong," said Joe.

They laughed again.

"How do you think I'll look in a uniform?" asked Joe.

"You'll knock them dead," said Jack.

"I'll pass you the surplus," said Joe.

But Jack was no longer smiling.

"I think I'll join up with you, Joe," he said.

"With your bad back?"

Joe referred to the back injury Jack had incurred in football scrimmage in the old days at Harvard.

"There's nothing wrong with my back!" protested Jack.

"Are you kidding?" said Joe.

"It doesn't bother me," said Jack. "I don't see why it should bother the Army!"

"They'll never take you," said Joe, and it was to seem for a while that he was right.

"Sorry," they said at the Army Recruiting Center, despite the growing need for men.

"What's wrong with me?" demanded Jack. "My vision is good. There's nothing the matter with my legs."

"Your back."

"My back's fine."

111

"Not for us. Sorry."

"Sorry!" stormed Jack. "I can walk as well as anybody you've got in camp! I can march as well as anyone else. I can take orders!"

"Sorry."

"Sorry!" Jack scowled, and he stormed out of the Army Recruiting Center and hied himself down to where they were taking enlisted men into the Navy.

It wasn't any better for the eager would-be recruit with the men who run the sea lanes for the United States of America.

"Your back."

"What's wrong with it?"

He was ready to tear the doctors apart.

"Sorry."

"Sorry! The country is calling for volunteers. We're drafting men into the service every day of the week. What's this 'sorry' bit they're pulling on me!"

"They know what they're doing, Jack," said his father. "It's their business to build up a strong army and a strong navy. They seem to be doing a good job of it."

"Then you don't think I'm fit to serve either," challenged Jack.

"*They* don't think so, Jack. They haven't asked me for my opinion. I don't think my opinion would count anyway. Not in this business. Some other, perhaps."

Jack cooled off. He had no other course. Besides, he knew, despite his wishing that it were not so, the Army and the Navy were both right. His back had never been the same, never been what it ought to have been, after that football scrimmage in Harvard.

"I'm not going to just stand by," he said, "and let everyone else do the fighting. I'm not hiding behind a bad back, Dad."

"I didn't think you would," said his father.

"No," said Jack. "I'm going to fix it. I'm going to build up the back muscles. And I'll build up the muscles in my arms, in my body, in my legs. I'm going to be so glowingly healthy the next time I walk into a recruiting station that they'll be asking me where I've been all this time!"

Jack Kennedy never lacked for determination nor for the will power to carry through his plans. Once he had decided on a course of action, he stuck to it until his purpose was achieved.

"I've urged our country's participation in this war against

Hitler," he said. "I intend to participate, and in the front lines of the battle."

He organized a routine. He bought equipment, special equipment. At first his neighbors in Hyannisport were startled when they saw Jack reach for a tall limb of a tree, then swing himself up so that he might hang loose by his hands, his feet far off the ground.

"It builds up the back muscles," he had to explain.

The neighbors wondered at it, then got used to it.

"One hour a day," he said. "Try it yourself. You'll be amazed at what it will do for you."

There weren't many who tried it. It was too strenuous. It wasn't too strenuous for the young man who was determined to prepare himself for the service of his country.

"Where did you get all these heavy things?" asked his mother.

"Weights, Mother."

"What in the world are you going to do with them?" asked Eunice.

"Just watch."

At first he lifted the lighter weights, then the heavier ones.

"It develops the muscles," he said.

"There must be some other way," said Kathleen, and she tried to lift the lightest of the weights. "I'm sure you know what you're doing," she said.

"I certainly do," said Jack, lifting the weight he had chosen, raising it slowly over his head.

"You're working awfully hard at this thing," said Rosemary.

"It'll get me what I want," said Jack.

He hung by his hands from the limb of a tree, he lifted weights, he followed a routine of exercises to strengthen his abdominal muscles, and three and four mornings a week he donned his old Harvard track suit to run a mile or two or three before the run back home.

"Hungry?" his mother would ask.

First came the shower and some fresh clothes, then on the double to breakfast.

"Starved!" he announced, reaching fast for a hot roll.

"There's enough to eat," said his mother.

"And can I eat it!" said Jack, moving into the orange juice, the cereal, the ham and eggs, everything in sight on the table.

"I could eat enough to feed a small family," he offered,

113

and he did; then he washed it down with a couple of quarts of milk.

"Aren't you overdoing it, Jack?" asked Rose Kennedy.

"I've just got a healthy appetite, Mother," said Jack.

"I don't mean your eating," said Rose Kennedy. "I mean all this exercise you're doing."

"I'm doing all right, Mother," he assured her. "What's more," he added, planting a kiss on her cheek, "I know exactly where I'm going."

Meanwhile, Joe had finished his second year at the Harvard Law School and then left to enter the service. He was already in the uniform Uncle Sam provided for him.

16

Joe Kennedy, Jr., was up early this morning of mid-July 1941, but the family was already waiting for him at the table when he walked in to breakfast. He looked around at all the solemn faces, his father, his mother, his sisters, his brothers, and burst into a roar of laughter.

"What's all this gloom for?" he demanded.

"Not gloom, son," said Joe Kennedy, Sr. "We're just a bit more thoughtful this morning. It isn't exactly a picnic we're preparing for."

"Come on, Dad," pleaded Joe Jr. "'I'm just going off for a little spin. I won't be long."

"I hope so," prayed Rose Kennedy.

"Don't you worry, Mother," said Joe Jr., putting his arms around her. "It will all be over and I'll be back at Harvard before you know it."

The Kennedys, Joe, too, knew better, but they accepted the prophecy in good faith and made the most of it.

"You'd better have a good breakfast," said Rose Kennedy. "There's no telling what they'll feed you where you are going."

"Steak for breakfast, Mother," said Joe. "That's what they feed us where I'm going."

"And milk," said Kathleen. "Plenty of milk."

Rosemary laughed and Eunice laughed and Pat laughed. At least they tried to laugh. They tried laughing at anything that morning, but it didn't work. Joe Kennedy, Jr., was going into the Navy Air Force. There was no telling when he would be back. Perhaps he would never come back. Men go to the wars, but not all of them return. And Jack was doing all he possibly could to join the service. Soon, the family knew, there would be two Kennedys in the uniforms of their country. They thought all this, but they said nothing.

"Do you have enough warm clothes to take with you?" asked Rose Kennedy.

"It's July, Mother."

"It won't always be July."

No. It would not always be July. Nor would it ever be

the same in Hyannisport for the Kennedys after this July, 1941.

"I guess this is it," said Joe Jr. finally, getting up from the table.

Rose wanted her boy to sit there, where she could see him, just a while longer. It didn't make much sense; still it was what she wanted.

"Another glass of milk, Joe?"

"I've had all I can eat and drink, Mother."

They waited till Joe got his bags, then walked him to the door and across the lawn to his car.

"Good-by, Mother."

"So long, Dad."

"Jack. Eunice. Pat. Kick. Teddy. Bobby . . . so long, gang." He managed a smile.

"Take care of yourself, Joe," said his mother.

"Take care of yourself," said Rosemary.

"Take care, Joe," said Eunice.

"Write to us, Joe," said his father.

"I'll write. I'll take care of myself. Don't you worry any," he said, and he was off and away, bound for the Squantum Naval Air Base and the greater glory that waited for him.

There were seventy-eight other young men, college men, who arrived that morning at the Squantum Naval Air Base with Seaman, 2nd Class, Joe Kennedy, but there was only one man who interested the photographers and the newspaper reporters: the son of Joseph Patrick Kennedy, financier and ex-Ambassador of the United States to the Court of St. James's in Britain.

"Lay off, fellows," pleaded Joe.

He had known that there was going to be a lot of fuss, a heap of fanfare, surrounding his enlistment in the service. He had tried to avoid it.

"There are seventy-nine of us," he begged. "We're all in the same boat. We're all in the same uniform. Lay off it, will you, fellows."

There was no escape.

"It's good publicity."

"I don't want any publicity!"

"Uncle Sam wants it!"

"The people want it! They'd like to see a Kennedy in uniform!"

The commanding officer put in his appearance.

"What's all the noise?"

116

"We'd like a picture of Kennedy. We want a picture story on Kennedy."

"How about all the other men?"

"The Ambassador's son in uniform makes good reading," argued the reporters. "The Ambassador's son—no better, no worse than any other American, rich or poor—that makes good talk for the Navy! For the Army! For the services! We're still recruiting, aren't we?"

"It's good for the morale," urged another newspaperman, "good for the morale of the service, good for the morale of the people."

"Go ahead," said the Commanding Officer. "Go ahead, but take it easy on the man. He's just come up."

Reporters never take it easy, nor do newspaper photographers.

"Give us a smile!"

"Turn this way!"

"Here! Shake the C.O.'s hand!"

That was the easiest part of it.

"Why did you quit school?"

"Is there some girl you're leaving behind you?"

"Why the Navy?"

"Why the air arm of the Navy?"

"What did your father say about this?"

"Did he approve?"

"Was he against it?"

"Where does he stand on your enlisting?"

Joe Kennedy, Jr., except for those momentary bursts of anger, was always a pretty well-controlled individual. He had demonstrated his ability to stand up under pressure when he had stuck with James A. Farley at the 1940 Democratic National Convention. And he knew that, if never before, this was the time he could ill afford to lose his temper. He answered the questions as they came, quickly and briefly. He was not to be flustered by the barrage the newspapermen hurled at him. He even managed to keep a smile on his mouth for most of the interviews that first day at Squantum.

"There's no secret about this thing," he said.

"No?" said a Boston newsman. "Then tell us why?"

"I like the Navy," said Joe, smiling. "I've always liked the Navy. And I like flying and I like the ocean. Add them up: I enlist at a Naval air base."

Even the reporters had to laugh, with the rest of the recruits listening in.

"How about Harvard?"

Joe became a little more solemn.

"I'm in for the duration. When the emergency is over, I'm going back to law school for my degree."

"How about your future? Your future in politics, Mr. Kennedy?"

"This is my future right now," said Joe. "Right now I want to do my part, like everyone else, for my country."

He laughed off the question about the girl.

"Which girl?"

But he didn't laugh when the questions came to his family.

"They're all for it," he said. "They're all for what I'm doing."

"Your father?" pressed a newsman.

There had been a split between Joseph Kennedy, Sr., and President Roosevelt on America's foreign policy. Everyone in the country was aware of it. There had been endless articles in the press. The split had been elaborated on and exaggerated, even distorted.

"My father," answered Joe Kennedy, Jr., quietly but not without a touch of bitterness, "my father, especially, approves of what I am doing. He thinks I'm doing what I should be doing, and he's glad for it! Any more questions, gentlemen?"

Newsmen don't frighten easily, and sometimes their skins prove a little thick. There were no more questions, but they asked for and they got Joe Jr. up in a plane with Lieutenant Jack Dodge, and they got more pictures and more pictures; then they were gone, and Joseph Patrick Kennedy, Jr., moved into the earnest and serious business of training himself to become the best naval airman he could be for his country.

For thirty days he would train hard and long, going through the basic routines of a $54 a month seaman, 2nd class, at the Squantum Naval Air Base. Mostly, it was sheer physical exercise of a most demanding nature. A man in the service had to be at his physical peak. Joe, like all the other Kennedys, was accustomed to using his muscles, to keeping himself fit. The routines of basic training were somewhat different, somewhat more demanding, but his spirit was willing and his body was able. Joe Kennedy, Jr., was always to take his tasks in stride. He emerged from the grueling thirty days at Squantum a healthier, a more vigorous young man and a full-fledged Naval Cadet.

He was sent to Jacksonville, Florida. Here there was a more

rigid and a more taxing course. Here he would win his wings. Here he would be elected the president of the Cadet Club. Here he would be elected the president of the Holy Name Society. Here, most important, he would begin to fly for his country. He had pledged his life to his country. He was prepared to lay it down in the line of duty and in the service he had sworn to give.

In Hyannisport, Jack Kennedy continued to drive himself mercilessly in his campaign for physical fitness. His determination to serve his nation in its armed forces never wavered for an instant. He read the letters Joe sent home, and the weights he lifted were the heavier weights and the still heavier weights. He read the stories on Joe, stories that inevitably appeared in the newspapers and in the magazines, and he went out onto the lawn and hung by his hands that much longer from the limb of a tree. He ran three miles and four and five. Jack did not conceal the pride he had for his brother. He was proud of his every accomplishment. But it was Joe's uniform that Jack envied.

It wasn't the Naval Air Force Jack Kennedy particularly wanted to join, but as the months went by, he decided that some branch of the Navy could use him. So much of his life had been spent in the water, on the water, near the water. He loved the sea.

"It's where I belong," he said, and in September of 1941, he felt he was ready for the tests.

Of course he was prepared for the examinations. He was as physically fit as a man can be on his own training. Still he sweated out the hours at the Naval Recruiting Office, through the routine questions, through the less routine and very thorough physical check-up.

"You'll do," said the Naval officer.

"What do you mean I'll do?" asked Jack.

He had to have it sure. He wanted it spelled out.

"You're in the Navy," said the officer.

"Terrific," said Jack, utterly and completely delighted.

He didn't know whether to shake the officer's hand or salute him. He did both.

"When do I start?"

"You're pretty eager," said the officer in charge.

"The sooner I get into uniform, the better I'll like it," answered Jack.

He got the uniform, and he got an assignment. The sailor gear was fine and to his liking; his assignment was not.

Jack Kennedy was a writer, a successful author. The Navy

assigned him to a desk job in Washington, a writing job. He was to help put out a newspaper for Navy officers. It was not what Jack wanted.

"I belong on a boat," he said. "I belong on the sea. I want active Naval duty. Writing for a Navy paper is all right in peacetime. Now there's a war going on!"

"We're not at war," said the Naval officer quietly, after listening to Jack's complaint. "We're still at peace, and we think you're doing what you can do best."

Things changed on December 7, 1941. Out of the sky over Hawaii came Japanese bombers. Out of the sky, bombs rained down on an unsuspecting fleet of U.S. Navy ships anchored at Pearl Harbor. In a matter of minutes, without a formal declaration of war, without any warning at all, in one of the most nefariously treacherous acts in all history, the war lords of Imperial Japan attacked and destroyed a significant number of United States Navy ships, lives, and equipment, and our country was hurled into the thick of the blood and thunder of World War II.

"What good am I doing here?" demanded young Jack Kennedy. "Anybody can do this paper job! I know boats! I know how to run them! I've been around boats all my life, and you've got me glued to a desk job you can give to any landlubber you've got in the Navy!"

The Navy listened, but it didn't do anything, not for Jack Kennedy. For almost another year, he had to sweat it out in Washington and on a defense project in the South. But at the end of 1942, much to his relief, Jack finally got what he wanted.

"You'll report to Melville in Rhode Island," said the Navy officer.

"Another newspaper?" asked Jack skeptically.

"Motor Torpedo Boat Squadron," said the officer.

Jack wanted to let out a whoop. He couldn't. It wasn't Navy protocol.

He looked at his typewriter, at the sheet of paper with its story half finished.

"Someone else can write the last paragraph to this," he said, picked up his cap, saluted, and was on his way. At last, Jack Kennedy was going to see what he called "active duty."

Desk jobs will soften up a man, but Jack had taken precautions. He never let up on his exercises. He never gave up the weight-lifting, the running, the exercises for his back, for his abdominal muscles. Still, he wasn't as fit as he had been the day the Navy accepted him into its service, and

"Grapes," the toughest physical instructor at the Melville Motor Torpedo Boat base, was a man without mercy when it came to getting his sailors into top condition.

"I'm going to drill you and work you until you're a bunch of dried-out grapes!" he yelled at the men as he scowled up and down the line.

"That's why they called him 'Grapes!'" said Jack later. "And he really drove us, and he really dried us up!"

Yet these were young men at the base, and young men snap back from their fatigue quickly.

"How about a game of football?"

"Grapes" was off the field. Time for a little fun.

Quickly they had divided themselves into a couple of teams and were ready for the kick-off.

"Do you mind if I get into it?"

It was the tall, lean youngster, Jack Kennedy. He still looked like a youngster, though he was already twenty-five years old.

Paul Fay, who became Under Secretary of the Navy in 1961, was another of the recruits at Melville, Rhode Island, at the time.

"He looked like a sixteen-year-old high school kid," says Fay, recalling the incident. "Besides, he looked a bit too arrogant for the rest of us. Of course, we didn't know he was Jack Kennedy and, for a long time, none of us knew he was the author of 'Why England Slept.' We just didn't take to him at first sight."

But the Navy is the Navy, and if a man wants to get into a game, he gets into it, even if he is wearing a heavy wool sweater with his college "H" on it.

"The sweater was inside out," said Fay, "but you could see the letter plain anyway."

Jack sensed the antagonism, but he wasn't going to let it get in his way. He wanted to play, and he knew, once the game got under way, they would look at him differently.

"Why don't you get on that other team," said Fay, and Jack did. Fay was sorry faster than he would have cared to admit.

"Atta boy, Jack!"

"That was catching it!"

"Good run, Jack!"

"Good boy!"

He was all over the field, and all at once Fay's team was taking a real shellacking.

"Let's run this next play right over that kid," said Fay in the huddle.

It didn't work.

"I'll take him out myself in this next play," said Fay.

That didn't help either.

"We tried all afternoon to knock Kennedy out of the game, but he was smart, fast and shifty," said Fay. "He knew that we were trying to give him the business, but we couldn't block him out of a single play. As a matter of fact, a couple of times that afternoon, he pulled the brakes on me, blocked me out hard, and knocked me flat on my back. He was a good ball player all right, even if he didn't look any older than a high school kid."

That was play. Later on there was going to be another meeting between Jack Kennedy and future Under Secretary of the Navy, Paul Fay. It was in the South Pacific. Fay was an ensign, Jack a lieutenant.

Fay had wanted to be transferred to some other unit than the one to which he was assigned. He kept going from his own boat to another, trying to accomplish his mission. It wasn't a very fruitful task he had taken on, and at one point he delayed the scheduled activity of his squadron some ten minutes by his shuttling from ship to ship. When he finally returned to his own boat, an angry Lieutenant Kennedy was there to greet him.

"If you can't live up to the rules and regulations of this outfit, Mr. Fay," snapped the lieutenant, "something is going to be done about it. You're ten minutes late. Multiply that ten minutes by 7,000 men, and we've lost 70,000 minutes to the enemy. You can lose a war in less time than that. Now let's get on the ball and keep moving!"

Paul Fay was impressed, as any seaman would be impressed. The bawling out he got cleared a lot of the heavy atmosphere between the two men. Fay was to become a close and loyal friend of his lieutenant, Jack Kennedy.

But that was still all in the future in the spring of 1943. The business at hand was the training for active war duty, and Jack Kennedy attended to the business at hand. He completed his basic instruction with honors. He was commended for his handling of ships. Personally, he was rated "willing and conscientious." He was shipped to San Francisco. From San Francisco, he was sent into the area of the Solomon Islands. He was assigned as the commanding officer of a PT boat. In the summer of 1943, he became part of the now historic counterattack against the Pacific enemy, Japan.

17

Kohei Hanami, commander of the Japanese destroyer *Amagiri*, peered into the dark Pacific waters. Things had not been going too well for the Imperial Forces of Japan these last months. The order was no longer "Advance." The order was "Hold" or "Retreat." There was a scowl on the face of the Japanese officer. The schedule of war was not going according to plans, Japanese plans. The Americans had seized the initiative.

"We are taking on too powerful a foe."

"How shall Japan defeat so mighty a nation as the United States of America?"

These had been the arguments among the Japanese officers, and Commander Kohei Hanami remembered them well, standing on the deck of his destroyer, scanning the wide and the dark ocean. That was before Pearl Harbor.

Then at Pearl Harbor, they had seemingly destroyed the American fleet in one great, sudden surprise attack. The Pacific was theirs. They could move at will, and they did, taking one island after the other.

That was long ago. The program of conquest had moved rapidly. The opposition had been feeble and inconsequential, following those first months after the quick attack on Pearl Harbor, December 7, 1941.

What if the Americans called it a sneak attack? What if a world might condemn the treachery of it? Japan was victorious. The critics of the strategy of the Japanese war lords were not among the Japanese.

That was in 1941 and in 1942. On the night of August 1, 1943, Commander Kohei Hanami was no longer so sure.

Japan had been defeated at the Midway Islands. Japan had been defeated in the New Britain Islands. Japan had been defeated at Guadalcanal.

"What magic does this United States possess that it can rebuild its fleet in so short a period of time? What power does this United States have that in the matter of months it can rise from a graveyard of ships to a powerful fleet of war vessels, powerful enough to drive back the Imperial Navy of Japan?"

The Americans now controlled the air. The Japanese could no longer launch an attack in the broad light of day. Their operations were now limited to night attack, and here, too, they were failing. They did not know the American fleet now possessed radar. Radar was completely unknown to the Japanese. All they knew was that even under the cover of darkness, their night raids on the shipping of men and munitions were being intercepted, turned back, destroyed.

Commander Kohei Hanami, once a confident officer of the Japanese fleet, peered into the darkness of the Pacific night, his mind troubled with endless doubts, his face a deep scowl of resentment and anger.

Then out of the darkness, and almost upon him, he saw the PT-109.

His face changed from scowl to determination. His mind moved from musing and meditating to action. The PT boat was a scourge among the Japanese ships. Small as it was, the PT raised havoc among the Japanese fleets, especially with their lines of communication. It was only a few days before that a fleet of eighteen Japanese bombers had been sent out on a fruitless mission to destroy the PT base in Rendova Harbor at Lumberi Island. Tiny, compared with the destroyer or with any other warship, the PT boat was the American ship most hated by the Japanese and their navy.

"PT boat!" shouted Commander Hanami.

The Japanese sailors were at their guns.

"Ram it!" ordered the Japanese commander. "Slice it in two!"

At the wheel of the PT-109 was Lieutenant Jack Kennedy.

He too had been peering into the dark night, scanning the dark waters.

"No moon. Not a star in the sky," said Ensign George Ross, standing next to his skipper. "I've never seen anything so black."

"See anything?" asked Lieutenant Kennedy of his ensign, who scanned the horizon with his binoculars.

"Not a thing. Black. Black. No wonder they call this Blackett Strait."

The PT-109 was running on one engine. It was important to muffle the motors down in these waters of the Solomon Islands. The Japanese might appear anywhere at any time. A ship didn't advertise its position to the enemy.

"All clear," said Ensign Ross.

It wasn't going to be clear for too long. They both knew the terrible silence of the South Pacific could explode without

124

a moment's warning. The Japanese were being hard pressed at Kolombangara. The Japanese Navy was sending destroyers to relieve the garrison. It was the job of the PT boats to intercept those destroyers, stop them from reaching their destination.

"Not a sign of them," said Lieutenant Kennedy.

"Not a sign," repeated his ensign.

Earlier that night searchlights had been seen and gunfire heard along the southern shore of the Kolombangara coast. Lieutenant Kennedy watched and listened. It was important to know whether the searchlights and the firing came from the shore or from ships close to it. He had no way of knowing for sure, and there was no radio message from his base or from any of the other PT boats to help him figure it out.

He intercepted PT boat 162.

"Where are the lights coming from? Who's doing the firing?"

"It sounds like shore batteries," came the answer.

Still no one seemed to know for certain.

In wars, in battles, action is sudden and quick.

A series of staccato messages were heard by PT-109's radio: "I am being chased through Ferguson Passage. Have fired fish." "Well, get the hell out of there."

This was trouble. This was action. This was war.

PT boat 169 pulled alongside PT-109.

"Any orders?"

"I haven't heard," said Jack.

PT-162 pulled up alongside the Kennedy ship.

"Anything from the base?"

"Not yet," said Jack.

Their motors were cut down. The three commanders were at their wheels. Orders might move them anywhere. They were prepared.

"It's coming!" shouted the radioman on the PT-109.

"Go ahead!" ordered Jack.

"Resume normal patrol station," said Sparks.

"Resume normal patrol station," repeated Jack, and with the PT-109 in the lead, the three boats headed back to their assigned positions.

There were many myths about the PT boats during and even after the war.

"Those motor torpedo boats can hit a speed of seventy miles an hour. They launch torpedoes at a terrific rate of speed."

This was a pretty common manner of speaking about them. Actually, they could do neither. PT-109 was a plywood boat, built by the Elco Naval Division of the Electric Boat Company in Bayonne, New Jersey. It measured eighty feet in length, with three twelve-cylinder Packard engines, each engine capable of developing 1,350 horsepower. The boat could carry four 21-inch torpedoes and could mount four .50-caliber machine guns in its two twin turrets. It had one 20-millimeter mounted on the fantail of the boat, and of course its crew was equipped with the usual allotment of Tommy guns, Springfield rifles, and riot shotguns. The boat also carried an 8-inch blinker-tube searchlight and had a voice radio with a range of seventy-five miles.

The maximum speed the PT boat could develop, however, contrary to common gossip, was thirty-five knots an hour when fully loaded. After it had delivered itself of its torpedoes, it could run that speed up to forty-six knots an hour. It was not a super vessel, and its complement of three officers and ten men knew it, but it was a proud little ship and it had deservedly earned the fear and the hatred of its enemy.

For a moment, only a quick moment, the men of the PT-109 took the Japanese destroyer, the *Amagiri*, for a sister PT boat as it knifed out of the darkness of the Pacific.

"All men to your stations!" shouted Lieutenant Jack Kennedy.

He turned the PT boat to starboard.

This was no PT boat. This was the Japanese, and it was destroy or be destroyed.

"Fire all guns!"

"Fire all torpedoes!"

It was too late. There was no time.

On a line, holding its guns, full speed ahead, the *Amagiri* plowed into the tiny PT-109, and the PT-109 was sliced in half. A sharp knife couldn't have done better with a loaf of bread.

"Banzai!" yelled the Japanese commander, keeping straight to his course.

"Banzai!" yelled his Japanese crew.

In seconds, the gasoline tanks of what was left of the PT-109 ignited. One of the two segments of the ship caught fire, exploded, sank. Lieutenant Jack Kennedy was hurled against the wall of the cockpit. He landed hard on his back on the deck of what was left of his boat. For a moment he was completely paralyzed. He couldn't move. His mind was dazed.

He wasn't sure of what had happened. One thought hammered away at him in the noise and the furor of the explosion and the fire: "So this is how it feels to be killed."

But the body does not want to die, nor does the mind. Suddenly, Lieutenant Kennedy was in the water. He didn't know how he got there, nor would he ever know, but his arms were moving about, his legs were working away, and his mind was abruptly clear.

The sea was on fire all around him, but the bow of the PT-109 was still afloat. The watertight bulkheads were keeping it from sinking—if only the fire in the water did not get to it.

"You all right?" he shouted to the men he could see clinging to the hull.

He swam through the waters, yellow and red with fire, and joined those on the hull, Crewmen John Maguire and Ed Mauer. Soon Ensign Leonard Thom, Ensign George Ross, and Crewmen Ray Albert and Gerard Zinser reached the hull too. Jack Kennedy began to shout into the darkness, hoping there were others who had survived the ramming of their boat. His head was clear now.

"Hey there! Anybody out there?"

Voices came back to him out of the blackness of the Pacific.

"Over here!"

"Here I am!"

"I need help!"

Charles Harris and Pat McMahon were about one hundred yards southwest of the hull, Bill Johnston about a hundred yards to the southeast.

"I'll go after Harris and McMahon," said Jack, plunging into the water.

Ensign Thom moved out for Johnston. Ray Starkey, who was clinging to some debris, made it to the boat by himself.

Pat McMahon was badly burned. He had been the only man below deck when the Japanese destroyer struck. He had been in the half of the boat that caught fire and sank.

"I don't know how I got out of the boat," he said. "Only the Old Boy upstairs will ever know."

His head had burst through the lining of his crash helmet. "It feels like it's going to explode," he said.

The salt water entered his wounds and burned like acid. He bit his lips and took the pain, but he was utterly helpless.

"We'll swim you back to the hull," said Jack.

The fire in the waters had died out, but McMahon knew he wasn't going to be able to help his would-be rescuer.

"Keep a stiff upper lip!" commanded Lieutenant Kennedy.

It took him more than an hour, but he towed Pat McMahon to the still floating hull of the PT-109.

When Jack got back to Harris, Harris was all in.

"No use," he said. "I can't swim. Can't make it."

"For a guy from Boston," snapped his commanding officer, "you're putting on a great exhibition out here!"

Harris was discouraged, but his pride had been touched. He was a man from Boston after all.

"Just hold me up for a second, Skipper. I'll take off this heavy sweater."

Kennedy grabbed Harris and held him above the water while Harris shed his sweater and heavy shoes. Then he found that he could move more easily through the water, and he and Jack made it slowly to the boat.

Marney and Kirksey, the other two men of the crew, were lost. They disappeared and were never heard from again, two more of the many brave men who gave their lives for their country.

It was three hours now since Commander Kohei Hanami had crashed his destroyer through the PT-109. The two sister PT boats had seen the waters go up into flames, had sighted the wreckage, and had drawn the one, the normal conclusion. The PT-109 had gone down into the depths of the Pacific, and all its crew were dead. On shore, back at their base, there would be the memorial services, the last gesture to their gallant comrades, to the brave men who, they thought at the time, had been killed in the line of duty.

But, except for the two who had died, the crew of the PT-109 were very much alive. McMahon was badly burned, Starkey and Zinser had been burned also, Johnston had inhaled too much of the gas fumes, and Harris had hurt his leg, but their numbers were not up.

"What do we do now, Shafty?"

Shafty was what the crew had nicknamed its commander.

"Give me a minute to think," said Lieutenant Kennedy.

No one, of course, knew that the blast, which had hurled the skipper to the deck, had also cracked away at his old back injury, the injury that had almost kept him out of the service.

"How would we know?" they asked later. "He swam in that water for hours. He rescued two men on his own, then rescued us all. He never said a word."

128

"Sure there was lots of groaning, but not from Lieutenant Jack Kennedy!"

"How about PT-162?" asked Ross.

"Probably at its station," said Jack. "PT-169, too."

"How about using our Very pistols?" asked Ensign Thom.

"It would let them know where we are," said Jack, "if we fired them. It would also tip off the Japs."

"I can't hear anything," said Bill Johnston.

"I haven't heard anything for the last three hours," said Zinser.

"That means nobody is around," Harris deduced.

"Nobody," said Jack. "No enemy and no friend."

The black of the night was giving way to the gray of the morning. They could begin to see more clearly around them. It didn't help. They were the survivors of the sinking of the PT-109, hanging on to its hull, with only the big broad waters of the Pacific around them.

"The hull is taking on water," cautioned Ensign Ross.

"I know it," said Kennedy. "We'll have to act fast."

"The hull is sinking," said Ensign Thom.

"Sinking fast," said Lieutenant Kennedy. "We'll have to move fast."

He looked at his men, the able men, the good swimmers, the men who couldn't swim too far or too long, and the men who were injured.

"We'll have to swim for it," he said.

"How?"

"Where?"

"The hull is going down fast! We swim or we go down with it!"

The light of day was coming up fast.

"We can't all make it, sir."

"We'll make it," announced their commander, "and we'll make it together!"

The wounded men looked at each other.

For a moment no one spoke a word.

"Those of you who can't swim make it easy for those who can to help you," said Lieutenant Kennedy, breaking the silence. "We'll swim south and west."

"North and east of Gizo Anchorage?" asked Thom.

"That's what I figure," said Kennedy.

"It's about four long miles."

"Just about," said the superior officer.

"There are other islands," suggested one of the men, "less than four miles."

"Sure," said Kennedy, "and maybe they're infested with Japanese. We're not walking or swimming into a trap. We're gonna get to a nice, cozy, protected island. Then we'll see."

"Right, sir."

"All right, men!"

He took his last look at the sinking hull. It was no more than a foot above the water.

It was good-by to the PT-109. A man becomes attached to his ship. His ship becomes part of him. It was like part of him dying, the death of the PT-109. But this was no time for thinking about it, no time for weeping, lamenting. It was time to move out into the waters of the Pacific with their own arms, their own legs, their own bodies. It was now or never!

★ ★
18
★ ★

"Ready?" snapped Lieutenant Jack Kennedy.

"Ready!"

A huge plank of wood, once part of the gun mount on the PT-109, floated loose.

"Hang on to it, you fellows!" ordered Kennedy, indicating the men who couldn't swim and the poorer swimmers. "Hang on and push! It'll hold you for a hundred miles if you keep your heads up! Use it like a raft."

McMahon wasn't going to be able to push anything. He was in too much pain. He had managed to keep out of shock, but the burns had weakened him.

"Go ahead," he said to his mates. "This is as far as I can make it."

But Lieutenant Kennedy had other plans for him. While his crew looked on with the pride a man can feel but can't speak, their skipper calmly loosened the life jacket McMahon wore, pulled out two long straps, put the straps in his mouth, and started to tow the injured seaman to the port of their destination.

"Come on!" he ordered.

He watched as the men took off. Those who could swim were clear of the plank, the others pushing the plank before them, those unhurt aiding the wounded; then he bit his teeth hard into the straps of McMahon's Mae West and pulled away into the waters of the Pacific.

Stroke and stroke they moved, their eyes alert for friend or foe.

"You'd think they'd come looking for us!"

"The Imperial Navy of Japan?"

"Save your breath, fellows!"

"Is that a ship?"

"Not even a cloud!"

"We'll make it, fellows!"

For four hours they struggled in the water, tiring, tired, with their commanding officer leading the way.

"How much more?"

"Where's the American Fleet?"

"Keep going, men! Keep going!"

And there it was, a cloud, a shadow, land!

"Land!"

"Land!"

"Whose land?"

There were half a dozen small guns among them, small knives, a searchlight.

"If it's the Banzai boys," began Ross.

"We'll take the island from them!" snapped Thom.

Japanese or American, there was no choice now.

"Let's get there first," ordered Jack Kennedy. "We'll tackle whatever we have to when we get there."

For four hours they had battled the Pacific waters. It was fifteen hours since their PT boat had been split in two.

Slowly the shore grew clearer. They could define its shape, the foliage on it. Slowly and yet more slowly, cautiously, lest they wake an enemy, they moved to the island. Then there was sand. Their feet could touch the bottom. They flung themselves onto the dry land and lay still there, their breath coming hard, then softer and softer; and their need was for sleep.

Jack Kennedy had a moment for reflection, a moment for prayers. He had had no thought but of the immediate danger and the need to meet it, the need to get his men to safety, the whole of the fifteen hours they had been in the water. Now came the sudden recollection of the men on the sister PT boats. Had they met with the destroyer that had cut the 109 in half? And the base? Had they already reported the crew of the PT-109 missing? How soon would they get word in Hyannisport? Hyannisport. The long summer days of swimming and sailing and the battles with his brother Joe. Where was Joe now?

They don't pay you prizes for coming in second best. His father had said that. There was the sudden glow of pride in accomplishment. His crew had come in first. The Pacific had lost.

His mother. If they reported him missing, his father would stand up to it.

"He's missing," he would say. "That means there is hope."

What would his mother say?

How long would they hold up that cablegram: "We regret to inform you that your son, Lieutenant John Fitzgerald Kennedy, is missing in action"?

There was another motive now for a quick return and a safe return to his base.

132

He looked around at his men. He checked with the injured.

"You guys are the greatest," he said.

Men from Illinois, Massachusetts, California, Missouri, Florida, from every part and section of the United States, Americans all, and their commanding officer was proud of them.

"We did it!"

"You're an O.K. guy yourself, Shafty," said the injured McMahon, said every man of his crew.

"Wait till I get you back to the base," said Kennedy. "Tell me how great I am then."

He was up on his feet now. The island seemed deserted.

"Nobody home," said Ensign Thom, reading his superior officer's mind.

"Looks that way," said Jack.

He scanned the water for anything resembling a ship. There was nothing in sight.

"Let's see what kind of menu they serve up on this island," he said.

It was a small island. It didn't take him long to get back to the men.

"Coconuts," he said.

That was all they would have to eat. They weren't going to last very long if they were to be marooned on this desolate spot in the Pacific.

"Take charge!" he ordered Ensign Thom.

It was early evening. There was still enough light.

"I'm going to swim into Ferguson Passage. The Petes should be moving into their patrol areas."

The Petes were the PT boats, and Jack needed to sight one to get his men home safely.

Thom knew how tired the skipper was. He wondered quietly whether he could make it. He said nothing as Jack Kennedy slipped back into the ocean.

The lieutenant swam about a half mile southeast, reached a coral reef of an island, and walked along the reef, the coral cutting into his feet, until he came to the end of the island. Ferguson Passage was there before him, but the Petes he wanted to find so desperately were nowhere in sight.

Farther out on the horizon, sudden bursts of fire lit the sky.

"Anybody there?" yelled Jack to himself.

There were aircraft flares. The Petes were operating in Gizo Strait. The flares were from enemy planes. Nobody would be moving into Ferguson Passage that night. Jack began his return journey to his men.

Slowly but deftly, he moved through the water. He was tired. He was very tired. Suddenly, the pull of his arms, the kick of his feet, gave way to a swelling current. The harder he pushed, the harder he pulled, the quicker was the current against him.

"Ross!" he shouted out into the darkness.

"Thom!"

Nobody could hear him. The current had him in its tow.

"This is it," he thought, thinking it was all over for Jack Kennedy, but he lashed out against the tide with all of the little energy left in his body; it was no good.

He closed his eyes, said the prayer he remembered, passed out.

The current took the unconscious Jack Kennedy into Blackett Strait for about two miles and back again into the middle of Ferguson Passage, his Mae West life jacket keeping him afloat.

The miracle, of course, was that his head had not dipped into the water. Jack opened his eyes. The night was black. He could barely make out the shoreline in the darkness. But he was alive.

Fiercely, he beat out against the water. With the last of his strength he made the coral reef. He lay down, he thanked God, and he fell asleep.

With the morning, he swam the mile and three quarters back to his crew, completely exhausted, a fever burning in his body, and again he slept, slept through most of the day.

August 3. No rescue boat in sight. Nothing. . . . Nothing.

On the night of August 3-4, Ensign George Ross prepared to swim into Ferguson Passage.

"Maybe the Petes will be coming this way tonight," he said.

"Go to it," replied his lieutenant, "but watch out for that current. It's treacherous. If you don't intercept a Pete, maybe you'd better sleep on an island, come back in daylight, avoid the current."

The fever had subsided, but the men were getting hungry. Their diet of coconuts was giving way.

"Find me a PT boat," he prayed.

But Ross had no better luck than Kennedy.

"Nothing," he reported the next morning. "Not a thing."

"We'll have to be pushing out of here," said Lieutenant Kennedy.

"Where to?"

"We want to get nearer Ferguson Passage. We want to get something to eat."

"How?"

"The way we got here. Only there won't be so far to swim for it."

The tide was rough, the current strong, and the men that much weaker for their ordeal; but again it was Kennedy tugging McMahon, his teeth fixed in the straps of the Mae West, the old plank of wood supporting some of the men, and the able helping the injured.

They got to a larger island, Olasana, with more brush for protection and a fresh supply of coconuts, and no Japanese aboard. The survivors of the PT-109 slept soundly that night. In the morning, Lieutenant Kennedy had plans.

"Ross," he said to his ensign, "we're going to swim to Nauru Island. You and I. See what we can find. Food, boats, anything."

"It's a pretty big island, sir," said Ross, "the way islands go around here."

"You think we might meet some friends there?" asked Jack.

"Enemy, sir."

Above their heads and out of the clouds, three planes zoomed in the sky.

"Hey!" shouted Ensign Thom.

They were too high to see the lonely band of men on the small island.

"P-40's," said Ross.

"New Zealand planes."

One of the fighters broke away from the squadron.

"They've spotted us!"

It was something else it had spotted.

"He's over Nauru Island!" said Ensign Ross.

The plane zoomed low. They could hear the stutter of its machine guns.

"Japs on the island," said Thom.

The plane rose into the sky, moved on, was lost from sight.

"We're going to Nauru Island," said Jack Kennedy.

"How about the Japs?" asked Ensign Thom.

"We'll keep away from them if we can. Ready, Ross?"

"Good luck!" yelled the men on the beach, and the two officers walked into the water and began their dangerous mission.

"Into the brush!" snapped Jack, as they reached the island.

Ross was with him.

"Hear anything?"

"Nothing."

They made their way through the heavy foliage to the eastern shore. They peered out on the sands of the beach.

"See that box out there?"

"Japanese, I think."

Jack Kennedy moved quickly. He had the box and was back in the brush.

They opened their find.

"Candy!"

There were about forty bags in all.

"This is going to be a lifesaver!"

Farther up the beach, they found a canoe and a barrel of water.

"Hey!"

"Quiet! You'll frighten them away!"

It was too late. Two natives in a canoe turned their boat and paddled away.

"Must have thought we're Japs," said Ross.

"Never mind," said Jack. "We've got a boat, candy, and a vat of water. We'll have a feast with the rest of the guys."

Back at Olasana Island, Thom, who had been left in charge of the crew by Kennedy, had the men resting in a patch of brush near the edge of the beach. They were anxiously awaiting the return of Kennedy and Ross from nearby Nauru Island.

Suddenly the men were stunned to see a canoe approaching with two men.

"They're Japs."

"No, they look like kids."

"Hey, they're natives."

The men were beginning to panic when Thom boldly stood up and walked easily to the water's edge. He beckoned and shouted to the strangers, "American," Thom yelled. "No Jap—American."

The natives were amazed at the sight of the ragged blond giant and at first were frightened and paddled furiously away.

Then Thom cried, "White star—white star." He pointed skyward as he spoke, and the natives, finally understanding that "White star" meant the insignia of American planes, paddled in to the beach.

Back at Nauru Kennedy packed up the candy and water, made a paddle out of a slat of wood, told Ross to stand by, and paddled back to Olasana. He was surprised and delighted to see the two natives but did not realize they were the same two men he and Ross had seen at Nauru.

Kennedy distributed the candy and water and then pushed off once more to Nauru Island for Ross.

19

Lieutenant Kennedy and Ensign Ross paddled the canoe against the strong currents of the water in Ferguson Passage.

"I don't see a thing."

"The Petes will have to come through here some time."

"Not today."

The wind had begun to whip up. Paddling the canoe became stiffer.

"Let's head for home," said Lieutenant Kennedy.

"That breeze is blowing up!"

They turned the boat around.

The rain started to come down. The sea began to rise.

"Pull!" ordered Kennedy.

"That's what I'm doing!" yelled Ross.

Against the rains, the wind, and the heavy sea, the men were practically helpless in their tiny craft.

"Pull!" shouted Kennedy, and a wave filled his mouth with water.

Ross was tossed onto his back by a wave. He lost his paddle.

The sea turned the boat one way, then another; the two sailors were completely helpless as the roaring Pacific hurled the canoe and the men high into the air and down again.

The canoe capsized and was swallowed by the ocean or tossed and smashed against a reef. The two men lay on the coral, where the waves had washed them, the water spilling like fury over their prostrate forms.

"You all right?" shouted Kennedy above the roar of the tide.

"All right," Ross yelled back.

They were on some island. They didn't know which.

"Better crawl to shore!" shouted Kennedy, "before you're pulled into the sea again!"

They crawled, painfully, over the sharp coral. The rain kept falling, keeping them soaked, but they were far enough away from the sea so that the waves could not reach them.

"O.K.?" asked Kennedy.

Ross couldn't hear him. He had fallen asleep, exhausted.

Jack Kennedy shut his eyes. He began his prayer, but he didn't finish it.

Some providence, once again, had moved in to save the lives of George Ross and Jack Kennedy, and both men slept. The next day, August 6, Kennedy and Ross found their men on Olasana.

The morning sun seemed to give Kennedy and his men new life. They sat around talking about how they could best send a message with the natives.

Kennedy and one of the natives paddled over to Nauru, and while there, Kennedy picked up a coconut and carved this message on the smooth side: NAURU ISLAND NATIVE KNOWS POSIT HE CAN PILOT 11 ALIVE NEED SMALL BOAT KENNEDY. He pointed toward Rendova and said, "Rendova, you go Rendova."

Meanwhile, back on Olasana, Thom also wrote a message on a piece of paper, a message indicating their position.

When Kennedy and the native rejoined the rest of the group, the two messages were then given to the natives, who started off on their thirty-eight-mile journey to Rendova.

Lieutenant Kennedy, his ensigns, his men, watched the natives until they were out of sight.

"Do you think they'll get there?"

"What if they're intercepted by the Japs?"

"We can hope," said the skipper. "We can pray. But we won't count on them."

"What do we do now?" It was Ensign Ross speaking.

"We go look for a Pete," said Kennedy.

If the two natives got to Rendova, they were saved. If the Japanese cut them off, it was the end of the brave little band marooned on the tiny coral island deep in the South Pacific.

Reg Evans was a coast watcher, a member of a special detachment of Australian troops who penetrated enemy territory, especially along the chain of endless islands in the South Pacific, and remained on those islands as the eyes and ears of the Allied Forces. The job required inordinate resourcefulness, self-reliance, strong nerves, and the kind of bravery that goes beyond the call of duty. The Coast Watchers of the Australian Army and Navy have yet to come in for the full share of honor due them for the part they played in the Pacific war.

Evans, in August of 1943, was stationed on Kolombangara, a small island across Blackett Strait. Like the other coast watchers of his troop, he had established himself in a well-concealed jungle hideout and had recruited a number of the anti-Japanese natives to work with him, scouting the enemy, their troop movements, their naval movements, their air maneuvers. Part of his job, and not the least important, was to spot the Allied airmen who might have survived a plane crash, sailors whose boats had been sunk under them, and to help rescue them.

The night the PT-109 was hit, Reg Evans had spotted four Japanese destroyers in his waters. The beam of one of the enemy ships lit up what he thought, at the moment, might be wreckage. There seemed to be some men in the water, too. He listened carefully. There were no cries for help. He could not throw his own beam; that would have exposed his position and helped nobody. He waited a while. There was no sound of human voices, only the muffled noise of the engines of the Japanese destroyers. He moved back to his hideout, removed the camouflage that hid his radio, made his report.

"Four Japanese destroyers. Some wreckage. It might have been just some flotsam."

It wasn't long, however, before Reg Evans got the facts on the wreckage and the men he had only thought he had seen.

"PT-109 missing. Thirteen men on board."

Immediately, the Coast Watcher went into action.

"A boat sunk by the Japanese," he explained to his native recruits and volunteers. Some of them could speak a bit of English, some none at all. "There were thirteen men aboard. They may have landed on some small island. Comb the islands. Comb the brush. Let me know what you find."

The natives dispersed in their native canoes.

Reg Evans went to his radio, his Tommy gun at his side. His Tommy gun was always at his side. There was no telling who would come calling next on his little hideout. It might be the Japanese.

"Search party organized." He spoke into his transmitter. "Will keep you informed. Relay any message."

The natives found a number of torpedoes washed on the beaches. They located the wreckage. There was nothing to report on the men of the PT-109. They were not to be found.

"Torpedoes," spoke Reg Evans into his radio sender. "Wreckage. Must be the PT-109. No survivors. Not yet."

There was always hope, considering the number of islands in the South Pacific, and the search continued.

"Nothing here," said Reg Evans. "We're still looking."

August 2. August 3, 4, 5.

"No news. Still searching. Moving to new area to search."

Hope dimmed for the survivors, if in fact there were any survivors of the PT-109.

"Looking. Looking."

Evans was sitting in the hut that was his hideout. He had just turned off his radio. He stretched. He yawned. It had been a long night. Suddenly, his hand went to his Tommy gun, and he was on his feet, alert .

The noise in the brush might be his native allies. It might be the enemy.

A dark head came through. Reg Evans relaxed.

"They've been found!" announced the young native.

"Who?" demanded Evans.

They might have found anything. They might have found anybody.

"Eleven!" said the native.

"Where?" asked Evans. "Eleven what? Eleven who?"

"Men from the ship," said the native.

Again, it might have been any ship.

"The PT-109?" asked Evans hopefully.

It could have been another ship. That wouldn't have been bad either except if it were a ship of the Imperial Japanese Navy.

"Americans," said the native.

Evans didn't need to know any more. If they were Americans, they were survivors of some sea disaster. He moved quickly into action.

"Where did you find them?"

The native explained. The two men on their way to Rendova had stopped to give them the news.

Evans pulled out his maps.

"Nauru Island," he said, pointing to the island on the chart.

The native nodded.

"Good work!" said the Australian Coast Watcher.

He pulled out a sheet of writing paper. Its heading read: ON HIS MAJESTY'S SERVICE. Quickly he wrote a note addressed to the Senior Officer on Nauru Island:

"Have just learned of your presence on Nauru Island. . . . I strongly advise you return immediately to here in this canoe and by the time you arrive here I will be in radio communication with authorities at Rendova and we can finalize plans to collect balance your party. Will warn aviation of your crossing Ferguson Passage."

141

He signed the note A. R. Evans, Lt., and ordered his natives to deliver it to the Americans.

Shortly after he cranked up his radio transmitter, contacted Rendova, and reported that eleven survivors had been located on Nauru Island.

A few hours later, the two natives carrying the messages from Thom and Kennedy reached Rendova, and then verification came through to Reg Evans—in the form of a radio message from Rendova—that the eleven men on Nauru Island were indeed survivors of the PT-109.

The men back on the island had no way of knowing, but their rescue might be close at hand. There was nothing certain, however, in the Pacific area in the year of 1943, and Lieutenant Evans counted the hours through the night, watching for the return of his natives with the Senior Officer they were to bring back.

Night moved into day, and Evans waited, waited, and waited. The sea was still. The air was still. All activities seemed to have ceased. The sun came up into the sky, and Lieutenant Evans was ready to give up his watch and wait for night to return again. The natives would know enough not to paddle their boats with an American officer visible to any enemy plane or ship that might spot him.

He slung his rifle over his shoulder, started the trek to his hideout, stopped, and turned to look for the last time that morning. There was a speck on the horizon. It might be a large enemy destroyer at that distance. It might be one of his boys coming in from one of the islands. He watched as the speck grew larger.

It wasn't a destroyer. He could see that now. He took his gun off his shoulder and held it in his hands. The speck was a canoe now. Now he could see that natives were paddling it through the water, the natives he had sent to Nauru Island. There was no American officer with them.

The Australian snapped a twig off a bush.

"Couldn't get through," he said to himself.

He couldn't conceal his disappointment; nor could he conceal his curiosity about the cargo of coconut leaves the natives were carrying in their boat.

He walked to the edge of the water and helped his boys pull the boat into the brush.

"What have you got here?" he demanded.

The boys didn't answer. They just started to pull the leaves out of the canoe, and there, well hidden from any possible enemy eyes, was their really precious cargo, Jack Kennedy.

"Evans is my name," said the delighted Australian.

"Kennedy," said the American.

They shook hands heartily.

"How do we get the rest of us off the island?" said Jack.

"We could canoe you to Rendova," said Evans.

"How about my crew?"

"You might pick up a Pete there on Rendova," suggested the Coast Watcher.

"No," said Kennedy. "I want to get to my men as fast as it is possible. Wire Rendova. Say I'll meet them anywhere they say, and I'll guide them to the island."

"As you say," said Evans.

For hours that night, Jack Kennedy waited in a canoe for a PT boat to pull into Ferguson Passage. This was the arranged rendezvous.

"What's keeping them? What's keeping them?"

Finally, the soft sound of the Pete, its motors cut down, approached over the waters. It cut through the darkness; it was there!

"Where the heck have you been?"

"Kennedy?"

"Kennedy!"

"We thought you were dead!"

"Well, I'm not! Let's get going!"

A muffled cheer came from the men as the Pete pulled in to the island. Then, "All aboard!" and the saga of the sinking of the PT-109 was almost over. All that remained was the report, followed by another report, followed by still another report. Then the citations.

"For extremely heroic conduct as commanding officer of Motor Torpedo Boat 109," began Admiral Halsey's citation, awarding Lieutenant John F. Kennedy the Navy and Marine Corps Medal, "following the collision and sinking of that vessel in the Pacific War Theater, August 1-2, 1943.

"Unmindful of personal danger Lieutenant Kennedy unhesitatingly braved the difficulties and hazards of darkness to direct rescue operations, swimming many hours to secure aid and food after he had succeeded in getting his crew ashore.

"His courage, endurance and excellent leadership contributed to the saving of several lives and was in keeping with the highest traditions of the United States Naval Service."

"None of that hero stuff" was Jack Kennedy's response,

however, to the eager reporters who saw a good news story in the heroism of Ambassador Kennedy's son. "None of that hero stuff about me," he said. "The real heroes are the men who don't get back, and you can include my two men among them."

He praised the surviving members of his crew.

"There was no beefing. Every man did his job. McMahon didn't complain once about his burns, and those burns were bad."

But his thoughts were with the two who hadn't made it, the two who had gone down with the PT-109.

There was another citation Jack received. This did not come with a medal.

"It's just like him," said Grandfather Honey Fitzgerald, not without pride. "He's got a lot of courage, that boy. It's just what we expected."

Joseph Kennedy, Sr., who had been informed that Jack was missing and had kept the news from the lieutenant's mother, from his sisters and brothers, always with the small hope that his son would be found, wired a simple but moving message.

"Thank God for your deliverance!"

20

The normal Navy procedure, following an experience like that of the PT-109's crew, was to send the men home for a well-earned rest.

"That's not the way I see it," said Jack Kennedy, turning the Navy leave down flat. "There's a war going on. Give me another boat. Give me another crew."

Squadron Commander Cluster looked the young lieutenant over.

"I know a lot of men who would give their eye teeth for this leave to go home and get a good rest."

"Give it to them," said Kennedy. "I came out here to fight."

"If you change your mind," began Lieutenant Cluster.

"Thank you, sir," said young Kennedy.

He saluted, turned on his heels.

"With men like that," thought Cluster, "how can we lose?"

He assigned Kennedy to another boat, the PT-59. He gave him another crew. But Jack's days in the Pacific were numbered.

For the first time since the sinking of the PT-109 and the ordeal of the rescue, the young lieutenant was aware of the old injury to his back. The blast, which had preceded the fire on the ship and hurled him flat on his back had brought alive all the old pain and made it worse. Walking, running, any physical activity, became a matter of will power over real and sometimes excruciating physical pain. In the heat of battle, in the fight to survive, the hurt and the handicap were somehow obliterated from his consciousness. Back in Rendova, the injury and the pain came on him full force.

"You're limping."

"I must have something in my shoe."

He straightened up, and, however painful, he walked without the limp.

"Something wrong?"

Despite himself, the pain made him grimace.

"Something I ate," said Kennedy.

He didn't want to be sent back to the States. He wanted to stay and fight. He might have continued the act and concealed the injury, as he wanted to, but the injured back collected an ally: malaria.

His condition became serious. When he lost twenty-five pounds, the C.O. took measures into his own hands and had Jack shipped back home.

"I know that this isn't what you want," said the Commanding Officer. "Come back to us when you're on your feet."

They still didn't know about the back—only about the malaria—or else they would have sent him to a hospital in the states. Instead, they sent him to Miami, Florida, to serve as an instructor in a PT training program.

"Put on that weight and get back to us," said the C.O. "We like you out here."

But Jack didn't get back to his old command. The back injury was getting worse, and he was doing nothing to help it.

Injury or no, pain or no, he kept hammering at his superior officers for a return to active duty.

"Send me to the Mediterranean," he asked. "Send me anywhere. You need a man like me where the shooting is."

It was no good. By May of 1944, he could no longer hide behind a smile or a painfully executed solid stride.

"We're sending you to the hospital, Kennedy."

"What for?"

"Because that's where you belong," snapped his superior officer, "if you want to get well and be of any real use to us."

Jack was past arguing. His officer was right.

"Where are you going to send me?"

"You're from Boston, aren't you?"

"Boston, New York, points east, points west."

He managed a painful smile.

"We're sending you to the Chelsea Naval Hospital. That's near Boston. It will make it easier for your people to visit you."

Chelsea Naval Hospital was near Hyannisport, too. The memories of his boyhood crowded in on young Kennedy: the swimming, the sailing, the fights with Joe, the races with Joe, his father, his mother, Rosemary, Kathleen, Eunice, Jean, Bobby, all his brothers and sisters.

146

"Time doesn't just move quickly," he thought. "It whips past you like a wind."

There was some compensation for his being hospitalized. He was near enough to visit his family weekends, and the hospital permitted it.

"You've lost a lot of weight, son," said Rose Kennedy.

"I'll get it all back, Mother," said Jack, "especially the way you've been feeding me."

"It's good to see you," said his father, "though I never did believe for a minute that you had been lost in the Pacific."

"It doesn't happen to us Kennedys, does it, Dad?"

"I hope not. I pray not."

His prayers for Jack had been answered.

"I'd like to see Joe home, too," said his father. "I'd like to hear you two battle again. That would make sweet music for my ears."

"He'll be home, Dad. He'll be home soon," said Eunice. "And you'll be asking them to lower their voices and to be a little more rational in their arguments."

Joe Sr. smiled, but there would never be another argument between the two brothers, no more battles, no more races, no more anything. Joseph Patrick Kennedy, Jr., was not coming home.

Joe was attached to a squadron of heavy Liberator bombers operating out of England. The job of the squadron was to hunt, harass, wreck every submarine they could spot in the Bay of Biscay.

"He's the best pilot in the squadron," his superior officers said, but Joe wasn't happy with his duties.

"I've been in the Navy three years," he said, "seventeen hundred hours. Three hundred in training. Six hundred in Martin bombers in anti-sub stuff in the Caribbean. Eight hundred in Libs. I'll still take carrier duty with a fighter."

He wanted more action. He wanted to get into the thick of the fighting.

"Things happen on carrier duty," he said. "I've made twenty-nine missions. The next one is my thirtieth. Do you know what happens after you've made thirty? You go out on your thirty-first. Give me carrier duty!"

It wasn't as easy as Joe made it seem. The B-24's didn't have the Bay of Biscay to themselves. They didn't encounter the kind of fighting that took place in the air over France, Belgium, England, Germany, but there was fighting, and there were casualties, of bombers and men, as the Nazi fighters came out to greet the American Navy airmen. Still, it wasn't enough for Joe Kennedy. The Kennedys never liked playing in the side show; they wanted to be right in the middle of the big event.

Joe got his chance.

His crew had been sent home on leave. He had turned down the leave himself, sensing something important was in the making. He was right.

It was August, 1944, just a year after Jack Kennedy had had his PT boat sunk under him, and the commanding officer of the base called in Lieutenant Joe Kennedy and Lieutenant Wilford J. Willy of Texas.

"This is an important mission, men," said the C.O. "You have your instructions. Good luck!"

The flight was over Normandy. Their ship carried a deadly message. It was jammed with tons of explosives and maneuvered by remote control. The plane, among the flying men, was called a "Flying Bomb." Its purpose was the destruction of a Nazi V-2 launching site.

"We hit the silk just as soon as they've got radio control of the boat," said Joe Kennedy.

The "silk" was the parachute.

"I've got it," said Lieutenant Willy.

"I've waited a long time for this," said Kennedy.

Willy just smiled.

"Action!" said Kennedy. "Action!"

"You've got it," said Willy.

"I've waited long enough," said Joe. He was at the controls.

It was a delicate maneuver. Project Anvil, the Navy called it. The idea was to develop a pilotless aircraft that was to prove an effective weapon against the deadly rocket bases of the Third Reich.

Officially, the Navy was to announce that its project called Anvil had been completed successfully. Two men were to give their lives for it.

Lieutenant Joe Kennedy had his plane high above the clouds.

"Everything O.K.?"

"They're coming now," said Lieutenant Willy.

He was speaking of the sister ships that were to take over the controls of the "Flying Bomb," remote control. Once they were in proper position, the two lieutenants would take to their parachutes and jump, leaving the rest of the squadron to dump the "Flying Bomb" on its target.

But the sister ships never did get into position, never did take over the controls.

Suddenly, there was one explosion, followed quickly by another, and the "Flying Bomb" was torn apart, shattered in mid-air. Its two pilots were killed immediately.

Static might have caused an electrical explosion. There was always the possibility of sabotage. A possible direct hit by flak, the electric heating of a fuse from some unknown source, gas leakage ignited by an electric spark—any or all might have been responsible for the tragic disaster. No one could ever know for sure. Two brave pilots lost their lives in the mission, Lieutenant Wilford J. Willy and Lieutenant Joseph Patrick Kennedy, Jr. This was the one fact the Navy could report.

It was August 2, 1944, when two priests called on Joseph Kennedy, Sr., at Hyannisport. Theirs was a solemn mission, and they asked to see Mr. Kennedy alone. Joe Kennedy, Sr., was gray when he emerged from his meeting with the two priests, and he could not keep the news from his family.

"Joe has been reported missing in action," he said.

It was just twelve months ago that Jack had been reported missing in action. Jack was home, spending the weekend away from the hospital with his family. The news hit him like a triphammer. He wanted to say, "They'll find him. They found me. They'll find Joe." But his mouth was frozen.

Rose Kennedy let the tears roll down from her eyes.

"God is merciful," she said.

"God is merciful," repeated Joe Kennedy, Sr. "Joe is alive. He must be alive."

But Joe was dead. He had paid the full measure of his devotion to his country. He would never come home again.

"For extraordinary heroism and courage in aerial flight as Pilot of a United States Liberator Bomber," read the citation signed by James Forrestal, Secretary of the Navy. "Well knowing the extreme dangers involved and totally unconcerned for his own safety, Lieutenant Kennedy unhesitatingly volunteered to conduct an exceptionally hazardous and special operational mission. Intrepid and daring in his tactics and with unwavering confidence in the vital importance of his task, he willingly risked his life in the supreme measure of service and, by his great personal valor and fortitude in carrying out a perilous undertaking, sustained and enhanced the finest traditions of the United States Naval Service."

Rose Kennedy received the citation and the Navy Cross

in a simple ceremony in the office of Rear-Admiral Felix Gygax.

More than anything else, Jack wanted to be at that ceremony. He couldn't. He lay in his hospital bed, wracked with pain.

Eunice, Pat, Rosemary, Bobby, twelve-year-old Teddy, visited with him, tried to cheer him up, and he smiled at their little stories, their little jokes, but the ache would not leave him.

An operation had been ordered.

"We'll have to get right down to the injury itself. It isn't a simple operation," warned the doctor.

But it was neither the incessant pains in his back nor the prospect of a serious operation that kept Jack from finding some comfort, some release in sleep. It was his brother Joe.

"I've lost my brother," he said to himself. "Joe is gone."

It ate into him; he had no appetite. It ate at his peace; there was no rest. It ate at his heart.

"My brother Joe. My brother Joe. My brother Joe is gone."

All the years he remembered, destiny had smiled on his family. Everything a Kennedy touched blossomed and bloomed. The story of the Kennedys was a long success story, with not a break in it. It was as if bad luck and misfortune were afraid of the Kennedys. Even in the South Pacific, what might have been disaster wound up in a blaze of glory.

Joe was dead. For the first time, tragedy had struck a blow at the happy family of the Kennedys of Hyannisport. It would strike again and quickly.

Kathleen, Joe's favorite sister, the sister he called "Kick," had married William John Robert Cavendish, the Marquess of Hartington. She had met him at an embassy ball in London. He had been nineteen then and she seventeen. He was an aristocrat, descended from a long line of British nobility. His family crest dated from the fourteenth century. He was Protestant. Kathleen was Catholic. It hadn't mattered. They had been married during the war.

"It's going to be a happy marriage," Joe Jr. had said, reporting to his family on the ceremony.

It had been, but the Marquess of Hartington was called off on military duty. Kick got the cable from home, saying, "Joe is dead." She raced across the sea to be with the family, and it was in Hyannisport that she got the second terrible cable, in a matter of weeks.

150

The Marquess of Hartington, Kathleen's young husband, had been killed in action "somewhere in France."

The Kennedys were deep in sorrow. Theirs was a close-knit family. The death of Joe, the death that had taken Kathleen's husband so soon, cut deeply.

"They were so young. They had everything going for them," said Jack.

Joe Sr., Rose, Eunice, visiting in the hospital, hid their tears and talked of other matters, but Jack brought them back to his brother Joe.

"He was so strong. Such a great friend."

"You look awfully thin," said Rose.

"Get well and come home," said Joe Sr.

"I'm going to write a book," said Jack.

"Let it wait until you're back on your feet," said Eunice.

"There'll always be time to write," said Rosemary.

"I'm going to do a book on Joe," said Jack.

"Forget it for now," said Joe Sr. "You need all the energy you've got," he said, but there was a lump in his throat, and he turned his face away to conceal his emotions.

The next time he visited, however, he brought some letters Joe had written to him, some letters of his written to Joe.

"Don't work too hard at it, Jack," his father admonished. "But I do like the idea."

Everybody was for the book now, and everybody wanted to help.

"Mostly it will be letters," Jack explained to Eunice and little Teddy. "Letters about Joe. Letters for Joe."

"I want my letters in there!" blurted twelve-year-old Teddy. He looked up to Eunice.

"I can have my letter for Joe, too, can't I?"

"Sure," said Jack, taking his brother's hand. "Everyone in the family will have a letter in it. It's a sort of good-by-to-Joe letter."

For a moment there was a silence, the silence and the pain of memory.

"How will I start the letter?" broke in Teddy, suddenly recognizing the burden he had assumed.

Eunice smiled.

"You'll know as soon as you get to write it," said Jack.

"But I never wrote anything like this before," protested Teddy.

"You'll say," began Eunice, "my brother Joe was so calm and so strong..."

"But he had a terrible temper!" cut in young Teddy.

He stopped. He was embarrassed.

"He did have a terrible temper," said Jack, "but that wasn't all of him, was it?"

"No."

"You write what you want to write," said Jack.

He did, and it was included as he wrote it, in the book Jack prepared in memory of his brother.

But letters from the family were only the beginning of the manuscript.

There were letters from Commander James Reedy, Commanding Officer of Joe's squadron in England, from Lieutenant Ted Reardon, Joe's closest and life-long friend, from Ensign Dick Flood, a friend of Joe's at Harvard and at the Harvard Law School, and each letter, as Jack read it, cut deeper and deeper into the pain of his knowledge that Joe was dead.

Dr. Payson Wild, Jr., Joe's adviser at Harvard, remembered Joe "bubbling over with energy, ideas and fun."

"I always felt," he wrote, "that he had ahead of him an extremely useful, distinguished and interesting career in some phase of public affairs. His charm, humor and good sense, added to his knowledge of basic factors and forces, would have carried him far. Instead of serving us so ably in peace, however, he served us in war. The rest of us are the loser but we shall never forget him."

Jack let the letter rest on his lap. His eyes closed and his thoughts wandered back to Hyannisport. He recalled the games on the lawn, the swimming, the sailboats. He remembered Joe chasing him along the breakwater, threatening his very life.

Harold J. Laski wrote of Joe's astonishing vitality, his enthusiasm, his immense energy and eagerness. He was glad that he and Joe had been friends.

Arthur Krock, Washington chief of *The New York Times* wrote, "If ability, integrity and courage are rewarded by the people, as I think they always are, he would have come to high place and never had cause to be ashamed of any act or word. . . . That was true of him in everything, as long as he lived, and in the manner of his death his life was exemplified."

Sorrow is tempered by such eulogies, but only tempered. The sorrow remains forever.

Jack finished the book. It was his homage to his brother. It was an expression of his love for him, of the love of all the Kennedys for their oldest son and their oldest brother.

Jack called the book *As We Remember Joe.*

His own tribute was:

"I think that if the Kennedy children amount to anything, it will be due more to Joe's behavior and his constant example than to any other factor. He made the task of bringing up a large family immeasurably easier for my father and mother, for what they taught him, he passed on to us, and their teachings were not diluted through him, but rather strengthened."

Harold Laski had teased Joe Kennedy, Jr., when they had been together in London, "about his determination to be nothing less than President of the United States."

Just how much of Joe's will was passed on to his brother Jack is not easily measured, nor can we measure easily how much of Joe's ambition Jack took on. Lying in his hospital bed, Jack Kennedy had much time to think about what he had done, on what he might do. If it was a political life he was going to choose, he did not say.

First, there was the operation.

Would he ever be well again?

The pain in his back was excruciating.

"How soon do you operate, Doctor?"

"Patience. Patience," said the doctor.

"Patience," thought Jack. "This is the whole of our stock. This is all we have with which to fight our sorrows."

It was a dejected Jack Kennedy in the Chelsea Naval Hospital, but he was a young man, a very young man, and a whole and great life lay ahead of him.

21

They operated on Jack's back. It was a delicate operation; it was successful, but it was months before the commander of the PT-109 could walk about without a cane, on his own, in his full strength. He was a lean young man and a long way from total recovery when he was retired from the U.S. Navy early in 1945.

"Where now?"

"Law school?" suggested Eunice.

"Have you thought seriously of teaching?" asked Eunice.

"You've done pretty well with your writing," said Pat.

Writing taxed the mind. Jack still had to nurse himself when it came to physical activity.

"I've got an idea," he said to his father. "I've got an idea on peace."

"Why don't you put it down on paper?" said his father.

It wasn't a thick book; it was more of a pamphlet. "Let's Try an Experiment in Peace" he called it, and he argued for a complete disarmament of Germany and Japan, for a pact among the leading world powers, Russia, England, the United States, for cutting down on armaments, once victory was secured.

World War II had taken a terrible toll in lives. The dead were to be counted in the tens of millions. The wounded were countless. So much that was good of life was destroyed. The world yearned for the end of all wars. The world yearned for peace.

In May, 1945, the great nations of the world convened in San Francisco. Their intention was to create an international body to secure that peace the world wanted. They were to call it the United Nations. The Hearst press, looking for a man out of the service to report on their efforts, turned to young Jack Kennedy, the man who had written the best-seller *Why England Slept*, and Jack was off to the West Coast. For the time being, his career was selected. He was going to continue to write.

"This conference from a distance," he wired his papers, "may have appeared so far like an international football game with Molotov carrying the ball while Stettinius, Eden, and the delegates try to tackle him all over the field."

He was asked to cover the conference from a serviceman's point of view. He wrote like a sportswriter. His language was fresh and colorful.

"No one can set himself up as a spokesman for the men in service," he wrote. "No one can say what the servicemen think. There are twelve millions of them, and they think and speak for themselves."

He was direct. He was honest. He was, more important for the value of his dispatches, a keen and competent observer and analyzer of the events on the spot.

"For the first seven days in San Francisco there has been so much jockeying for position."

"The stormy sessions of the first week have done much to clear the air. They have shown clearly the tremendous differences between the viewpoints of Russia on the one hand and the United States and Britain on the other."

"It is unfortunate that more cannot be accomplished here. It is unfortunate that unity for war against a common aggressor is far easier to obtain than unity for peace."

And again of the servicemen: "Youth is a time for direct action and for simplification. To come from the battlefield where sacrifice is the order of the day—to come from there to here—it is not surprising that they should question the worth of their sacrifice."

"We are commencing to realize how difficult and long the road is ahead," he wrote. "San Francisco is only the beginning."

And finally, deep from his faith, he wrote, "There is here, however, one ray of shining bright light. That is the realization, felt by all the delegates, that humanity cannot afford another war."

The sessions in San Francisco were wearing, often discouraging, but not without some promise for those who believed in the possibility of lasting peace.

"It can be won," Jack wrote. "The United States may yet win the peace, if it remains strong, firm and confident."

Young Kennedy was among the hopeful, but to hope was not enough; to write about it was not enough.

"Youth is a time for direct action and for simplification," he had written.

He ached to participate in the making of this peace as he had ached to participate in the war, not at its edges but in the front lines.

He observed the Russian Molotov, the American Stettinius, the British Anthony Eden. They were the men whose words became deeds. Here was thought become action. If the memory of his brother Joe turned Jack Kennedy to considering the possibility of a political career, his stint for the press in San Francisco, his working among the top delegates of the three big world powers, all but steered him at once into the political arena.

"It's interesting enough, watching. There's some sense of gratification," he said, "writing about the big men, about all this maneuvering. It's a lot more interesting being part of the game, doing some maneuvering on your own. It's like the difference between watching a football game from the fifty yard line and running a football down the field with the good blocking in front of you."

"You don't play on the Varsity the first time you get into a scrimmage," said his father.

"No," said Jack. "I guess I ought to know that. But this game is one game in which I'm going to get my letter."

His first opportunity came quickly.

Jim Curley, old party rival of Jack Kennedy's grandfather, Honey Fitzgerald, had been elected a member of the House of Representatives, but he wasn't too happy about it. Washington was a long way from Boston, and he missed his old bailiwick, his old friends and cronies. He took care of this situation by running for mayor of his home town and winning the election. This, however, left Boston minus a congressman, and a special election had to be called.

By accident or opportunity, Jack Kennedy was just home from his second stint for the Hearst press, covering the crucial national elections in England, and the fever of politics was with him.

"I think I've got a good chance to win this election," he announced to his family, as they began to move away from the dinner table.

"Which election?" asked Joe Sr.

The dinner talk had centered about the critical situation in the British Isles.

"I think I can win Jim Curley's old seat in Congress," explained Jack.

Joe Sr. looked at Jack. Jack still showed signs of his bouts with malaria, of his operation at the Chelsea Naval Hospital.

"Are you sure that's what you want?" he asked.

"It's what I want," said Jack.

"Congressman," murmured young Teddy Kennedy, full of wonder at the title.

"It's tough out there on the streets of Boston when an election rolls around," said Joe Sr.

"You're not trying to discourage me, Dad?" asked Jack.

"No, no," demurred his father.

"I remember Grandpa Fitzgerald used to have a high time of it, campaigning in the streets of Boston, Dad. I had a good time of it myself whenever he took me around on those speechmaking tours of his."

"Grandpa Fitzgerald could still do it if he wanted to," said Joe Kennedy, Sr. "He lived on that kind of battling. He loved it. It can be pretty ugly at times, Jack."

"You can't win a fight unless you get into it, Dad," said the would-be candidate. "You can't come in first unless you get into the race," he added, paraphrasing his father's own words.

Joe Kennedy, Sr., smiled.

"Go to it, son," he said, "and God be with you. God be with us all."

For a moment they were still, both father and son. The memory of Joe Kennedy, Jr., suddenly flooded the room in which they stood.

"I'm going to be President of the United States," Joe Jr. had said.

Joe Sr. had been ambitious for his first-born son. He was no less ambitious for Jack, but Joe Jr., from the very beginning, had been his political hope, and Jack knew it.

Joe Sr. sighed audibly.

"God be with you, son. God be with you," he repeated.

Grief stays with a man, but a man must not stay with grief forever.

"You'll win," said Joe Kennedy, Sr.

He smiled. He took Jack's hand, shook it warmly.

"One thing I'm sure of," he said. "You'll win!"

Of course he would win, but his friends thought he might try for a victory that wouldn't prove so hard to achieve.

"The Eleventh District is tough."

"The Eleventh District is rough."

"Why don't you go after a seat in the State Legislature first? Then make the stab for Congress!"

"The Eleventh District is mean."

"Sure it will elect Jim Curley every time he runs. Will it elect a Kennedy? Will it elect a Harvard Kennedy?"

The Eleventh District was principally a poor man's district. It was peopled by Irishmen, Italians, Chinese, a host of immigrants from all parts of the world. The things they had in common were the tenements they lived in, the factories, the freight yards, the dumps, which decorated the area. It was a rough, tough, hard-boiled district, tailor-made for the rough and tumble Jim Curley, a strictly Democratic party district that demanded a man who could speak its own language.

"You're taking the hard way into politics, Jack," his friends cautioned, but nothing was going to deter the ex-Navy man once he had made his decision.

"My grandfather, Honey Fitz, represented this district fifty years ago," he said. "I'm going to be its representative tomorrow."

He had written a speech, announcing his candidacy.

"Tune in on the Yankee Radio Network," he told his family and his friends.

It was on the Yankee Radio Network that Jack Kennedy made the first political speech of his career.

"When ships were sinking and young Americans were dying," he said, "I firmly resolved to serve my country in peace as honestly as I tried to serve it in war."

He was officially a candidate for the Eleventh District seat in the House of Representatives. It was going to be a tough fight and he knew it. He knew, too, that he was going to come in a winner.

There were ten candidates in the primary fight for the seat vacated by Mayor Jim Curley. Two of those candidates were seasoned veterans in the political arena, former State Representative Michael J. Neville and WAC Major Catherine E. Falvey, who had already served a term of office in the Massachusetts State Legislature. Winning the Democratic nomination meant, virtually, election to office. The primaries took on the nature of an all-out political struggle, and Jack set himself to the task immediately.

He was cruising in his car, scouting the neighborhood, when he saw Tony Galluccio, an old Harvard classmate.

"Hey, Tony!"

"Hey, Jack!"

"When did you get out of the service?"

"How about you?"

"Married?"

"Children?"

It was the usual talk of old college friends, except that Jack was running for Congress.

"How about that!" said Tony.

"How about it!" said Jack.

"Need any help?" asked Tony.

"All the help I can get," said Jack.

"Then I'm with you!" announced Tony.

"Fine!"

"All the way!" said Tony, and he meant it.

He collared John Droney, later District Attorney.

"Listen to this," he said, and he read from a statement Jack had made to the press.

"Each passing day brings to light the increased need for prompt and intelligent action in public service. Veterans are daily faced with new problems of employment, housing, and rehabilitation. The general public's needs are greater now than perhaps at any time in our nation's history. The demands of peace are more far-reaching and more complete than the problems of the recent war."

"He's not going to win the Eleventh with that kind of speech," said Droney.

"Listen! Listen!" insisted Tony.

He read on.

"The temper of the times imposes an obligation upon every thinking citizen to work diligently in peace, as we served tirelessly in war. Everyone who is able should do his utmost in these days of world and national progress to contribute his talents in keeping with his abilities and resources. It is with this feeling that I declare my candidacy for Congress."

"That's where I come in, I suppose," said Droney.

"You bet!" said Tony Galluccio.

And Jack Kennedy had another young man in his camp, to work for his election.

Red Fay of his Navy days, Ted Reardon, Joe Kennedy's great Harvard pal, Les Billings, Rip Horton, and Torb Macdonald, old friends of Jack—a small army of young and eager men—rallied around the young Kennedy. A couple of professionals were called in to help run the campaign, Joe Kane and Billy Sutton. The Kennedys never did anything halfway. Mark Dalton, a lawyer and a writer on politics, was named Jack Kennedy's campaign manager, and the fight was on in earnest.

The day began at fifteen minutes to eight. A light breakfast and Jack was off on a round of his district.

"I'm Jack Kennedy," he announced in any one of the many workman's restaurants on his beat. "I'm running for Congress."

"I'm Jack Kennedy," he said, walking into the shops and

the saloons. "I'm running for Jim Curley's seat in the House of Representatives."

"Too young for me," said someone at a gas station.

He had just passed his twenty-ninth birthday, but Jack always managed to look more like a college undergraduate than an active political campaigner.

"Rich man's son," said another.

It was a handicap to be a rich man's son in a predominantly impoverished neighborhood.

At first, the street corner rallies were a problem.

"You've got to speak their language," Jack was told.

He tried, but it wasn't easy. He remembered Honey Fitz at these street corner rallies, and he marveled at the ease his grandfather had displayed.

"Friends," he began. "I'm Jack Kennedy."

The crowd was not too large and restive.

"The poor little rich kid."

"Carpetbagger."

"He's only a boy."

But Jack Kennedy began to speak directly to the needs of his listeners, about their hopes, their ambitions, their desires. He spoke on the need for jobs, on the question of the rising cost of living, on the necessity for decent housing, on social security, on medical care.

His audience listened.

"He makes sense."

"He knows what he's talking about."

"He's all right."

He shook their hands. He ate spaghetti with the Italians of the district. He ate with chopsticks among the Chinese of the district. He talked the language of the longshoremen, the language of the housewives. It was strictly an unorthodox campaign, a campaign that had the professional politicians scratching their heads in wonder.

"Now he's running tea parties," they said, and looked for what he would do next.

Tea parties! That was what they were, and nothing more!

"Mrs. Rose Kennedy and her daughters invite you to tea at the Hotel Commander in Cambridge. . . ."

The letter was addressed to all the women constituents of the Eleventh District, and there was a huge turnout at the Hotel Commander, to be received by Mrs. Rose Kennedy and her daughters, Rosemary, Pat, Eunice, Kathleen, and Jean, and to hear about their favorite candidate for Jim Curley's old seat in Congress.

Wealthy or not, Harvard or not, the Kennedy women were gracious, and the women of the Eleventh District were impressed, delighted, and won to the cause.

There were more tea parties, smaller tea parties, and one or another of the Kennedy women was hostess. Each tea party was as successful as the one before it, and the women's vote was quickly and surely garnered for Jack Kennedy.

Still, the political bosses looked skeptically on the efforts of this small army of amateur politicans. The one exception, outside the Kennedy camp, was that old master of the political game, Jim Curley.

"How can he lose?" he asked, speaking of Jack's candidacy, "with that double-barreled name, John Fitzgerald Kennedy?"

Jim Curley shook his head.

"No, sir!" he said. "There's never been anybody who could top either one of them, Pat Kennedy or Honey Fitz, never! Why young Kennedy doesn't even have to take to the stump, the way his grandfather did. He can forget all about this campaign. He can just pack his bag and go down to Washington right now, or any time he feels like it."

These were encouraging words indeed, coming from a professional politician like Jim Curley. Nevertheless, Jack redoubled his efforts.

All day long he toured the district, his back still laced in a brace. He wore that brace for a long time after his operation in the Naval hospital, but no one except a few intimates knew of it. At night, he would remove the brace and soak in a hot tub, but even in the tub, he would continue his campaign business.

And it all paid off.

The day of the primaries, Jack voted, then managed to get away from everything and everyone and sat himself down in a movie house to see *A Night in Casablanca*. He needed the rest. He needed to be alone.

When he came out of that movie house, he had been elected.

Forty-two per cent of the district had voted for Jack Kennedy against the field of his nine opponents; 22,183 people had cast their ballots for the hero of the PT-109. He had received more votes than the combined votes of his nearest rivals, twice as many as Neville, who came in second, three times as many as Cotter, the man who came in third.

"They don't give any prizes for second best," he said to his father, recalling an admonition from his boyhood.

"I knew you'd do it," said Joe Kennedy, Sr.

Rose Kennedy was proud of her son.

She kissed him.

"This is only the beginning," she said.

Honey Fitz, Grandpa Honey Fitz, climbed up on a table, and the eighty-three-year old veteran of the political wars danced a jig and sang "Sweet Adeline," and all the young Kennedys, Rosemary, Eunice, Jean, Kathleen, Pat, Bobby, and Teddy, joined in.

Jack Kennedy was going to Congress.

22

Jacqueline Bouvier was at a small dinner party arranged by her friends Martha and Charles Bartlett. The place: Washington, D.C. The time: the spring of 1951. An added attraction: the Congressman from Massachusetts.

"He looks familiar," said Jacqueline Bouvier.

"Jack Kennedy?" said Martha Barlett. "He should. He's been living in Washington for over four years now. He'll be a senator soon, if I'm a judge at all. Attractive, isn't he?"

Jacqueline Bouvier smiled.

"You think I ought to become more interested in politics," she offered.

"I know you can do much worse," countered Martha Bartlett.

It was her turn to smile.

"I think you'll find the Congressman from Massachusetts rather interesting."

He was interesting. He was attractive. He was most charming. Nor was he entirely without a certain touch of Irish blarney.

His conversation with Jacqueline Bouvier, however, wasn't the flip speech that comes so easily in dinner-party talk. He was really taken with the well-groomed, beautifully poised young woman. He was taken with her beauty.

"A remarkable man," said Jacqueline Bouvier, speaking to Martha Bartlett of Jack Kennedy as the evening came to a close.

"I was sure you'd like him," said Martha.

"I think I'll have to begin to do some intensive reading in politics," said Jacqueline, whose interests had been previously concentrated in the arts. "I never knew politics could be so exciting."

Jacqueline Bouvier, Jackie, as her friends called her, was born in Southampton, Long Island, New York, July 28, 1929. Her mother, Janet Lee, was a society beauty, her father, John Bouvier III—Black Jack his friends called him—a wealthy stockbroker and as handsome as a matinee idol.

Jacqueline inherited the beauty and was afforded all the material advantages by her well-to-do parents.

She attended the finest girls' schools: the Chapin School in New York, Holton Arms in Washington, Miss Porter's School in Connecticut. She studied for two years at Vassar, a year at the Sorbonne in Paris, where she delved into the historical and cultural background of her French heritage. She completed her formal schooling at George Washington University in Washington D.C.

She was named, at eighteen, the year of her debut, the nation's outstanding beauty. She was an accomplished horsewoman and won prize after prize for her horsemanship. She had a thorough background in the arts and letters, and she spoke French, Italian, and Spanish fluently.

Of course a girl of such beauty and accomplishment was not without admirers. Suddenly, the tables were turned. Here was a man *she* wanted to pursue her, someone she wanted to encourage, and like any other woman, she wondered when he would call on her or whether he would call on her at all.

He called.

She was delighted.

"Dinner and theater?"

"Of course."

"I'll call for you."

"I'll be ready."

The dinner was good. The theater was good. The talk was even better.

"Let's go to the National Art Gallery together," said Jack, pursuing Jacqueline's interest in painting.

"You'll have to explain a little more in detail," said Jacqueline, pursuing Jack's interest in the framing of a bill for legislative action on civil liberties.

They went to the National Art Gallery together, and Jack learned about the masterpieces they looked at from Jacqueline. Jack went into detail about every important bill before the House of Representatives; and Jacqueline learned about politics from Jack.

There were more dinners, many more dinners. There was much theater, and sometimes it was the movies, especially when there was a good one, American or foreign, to be seen. Sometimes it was just a walk, and sometimes an evening at home. And always there was good talk, and Jack and Jacqueline grew close to each other, as people will, speaking their minds, their hearts, and their hopes.

"How long have we known each other?" Jacqueline Bouvier asked herself.

It was a matter of only weeks, a few months, and it seemed to her that they had known each other for years. She wondered from time to time how it had all happened and when Jack would ask the question she so often saw in his eyes.

"In due time," she said to herself. "In due time," and she smiled because it was spring in Washington and dinner had been so pleasant, and they had laughed so much during the evening, and Jack had spoken about running for the Senate, and she had teased him for being ambitious.

"I know you're handsome enough to be a senator," she had said, "but you are much too young."

But Jack was serious about the Senate, most serious.

"I think I can win the Democratic nomination," he said.

"You can win anything you set your heart on," said Jacqueline.

Jack looked at her quickly.

This was the time to ask the important question, the biggest question.

"If I win a seat in the Senate," began Jack, "do you think . . ."

He hesitated.

"First things first," he said to himself.

"I should love to be able to call you Mr. Senator," she said.

Jack grinned.

"I would have to beat Henry Cabot Lodge," he said.

"And Henry Cabot Lodge is a formidable opponent," commented Jackie.

"A most formidable opponent," said Jack.

He frowned.

"That isn't what bothers me," he said.

Jacqueline waited. She was patient.

"It's going to be a big battle."

"I'll be rooting for you," said Jackie.

"I know you will," said Jack.

He looked at the young woman who had grown to mean so much to him.

"It will be a long and hard campaign," he said. "All in Massachusetts. It means I won't be able to see you. I won't be able to see you for the duration of the campaign," he said finally.

They looked at each other for a moment, and their silence was eloquent.

"You're going to be very busy," said Jackie at last, breaking the silence.

"If I want to be elected to the Senate," said Jack.

"I should be happy," said Jacqueline, "if you are elected to the Senate."

And then he was gone, and Jackie was alone again.

This was the last of Jack Kennedy that Jacqueline Bouvier would see for months. The campaign against Henry Cabot Lodge, three times United States Senator and important leader in the prenomination campaign for Dwight D. Eisenhower, was going to take all the energy the young congressman from Massachusetts could give it. There would be little time for anything else in the life of the young and fast-moving John Fitzgerald Kennedy.

Lodge was a polished gentleman in addition to being a polished politician. An aristocrat, born of the Cabots and Lodges, two of the oldest and most respected families in New England, the seventh of the Cabots and Lodges to serve his country in its Senate, Henry Cabot Lodge was a good speaker with a good record, a most popular figure not only in his home state but also throughout the nation. In addition, with the whole nation heading toward a record vote for Eisenhower as president, it looked as if nothing could stop Henry Cabot Lodge from winning his fourth term in the upper house in Washington.

"There's no one in Massachusetts who could beat Lodge in a race for the Senate this year or any other year," said the political wise men.

"They're right," said Jack's co-workers in the Democratic Party.

"Maybe, and maybe not," said Jack. "Only one man will be elected," he added. "I don't run to come in second best."

"And if you're licked," cautioned his friends, "it could mean the end of your political career."

"I've no intention of losing," snapped Jack. "Are you with me or against me?"

"But, Jack . . ."

There were so many ifs and buts, and young Kennedy would have none of them.

"Let's be done with doubt. Let's be done with indecision. We've got a lot of hard work ahead of us, and none of this scare talk is going to do any of it."

Political wise men are generally wise in their knowledge of public trends and the way in which the people are going to cast their votes at the polls. They might have been completely right in their estimate of Henry Cabot Lodge and his strength in the state of Massachusetts. What they did not take into consideration, however, was that special element, that rare quality, that relentless determination and drive that, together, spell Jack Kennedy.

"He has never had a really strong opponent at the polls," said the young campaigner, speaking of Lodge's previous victories. "The idea that Henry Cabot Lodge is undefeatable is a myth!"

The attack, as expected, centered on the youth of Jack Kennedy.

"He's only thirty-five years old!"

"He's only a kid!"

He ignored the attack as irrelevant.

"When the founding fathers of our country wrote the Constitution of the United States," he declared, "they established age limits. I am five years beyond that age limit. There is nothing in the laws of our nation which demands a man must be in his middle years and graying at the temples before he can run for the Senate."

The young Kennedy said, "Let's get down to the essential differences between the men running for office and to their platforms."

He pointed to his record and once more tackled the issues of the moment, the issues facing the nation, the questions the voters wanted answered most, the doubts, the hopes, the fears, the will, and the wish of the electorate. Once more the amateurs took over for the professionals.

"Think we can beat Lodge?" Jack asked his brother Bobby.

"You don't think you can lose, do you?" returned Robert.

"I'm asking the questions," said Jack. "Do you think we can beat Lodge?"

"Well, if you're going to be that serious about it," offered Bobby, and he grinned from ear to ear, "as far as I'm concerned, I'm talking right now with the next Senator from Massachusetts."

Jack hesitated a moment.

"It isn't funny, Bobby," he said.

"I mean every word I say," said Bobby, suddenly firm and decided.

"Then how would you like to manage my campaign?" asked Jack.

"You mean that?" asked Bobby, for the first time a little unsure of Jack's intentions.

"The job is yours," said Jack, "if you want it."

"Want it?" shouted Bobby.

He grabbed his brother's hand.

"You know what?" he shouted. "You've just got yourself the best campaign manager in the business!"

And he was just that, the best campaign manager in the business.

Bobby Kennedy had served his term in the Navy, given up a commission so that he could serve as an enlistee on the boat named after his brother, the United States destroyer, *Joseph P. Kennedy, Jr.* He had been released from service just in time to lend a hand with Jack's first race for Congress. Then he went off to the University of Virginia Law School to complete his education for the profession he had chosen. He was working as a lawyer for the Department of Justice when Jack asked him to run his campaign, but he handed in his resignation immediately.

"Let's go!" he said. "We've got a job! Everybody is working!"

He was perhaps the youngest man ever to pilot a campaign for a seat in the United States Senate. He was only twenty-seven years old when he took on the job, hardly more than an infant as age is measured in the hard-boiled school of politics and elections. But he was good. He was earnest. He was untiring. More than all else, he had a genius for getting the vote out for his man, for his candidate.

"Every minute counts!" he announced, and he showed them how to use every minute of the campaign.

"Everybody on the job!" he ordered, and no one worked harder, longer, more unsparingly than young Bobby Kennedy.

Politicians were always coming into the Kennedy headquarters now for one reason and another.

"He's expecting us," they would say.

"You'll have to wait," replied Bobby.

"When do you think he'll be coming?"

"Within the hour."

"We'll wait."

They waited, they talked, they talked and they waited, and all the time the Kennedy headquarters was alive with the activities of its campaign.

"He's late," said one of the politicians.

Bobby glanced at him, then got back to his desk.

"Half an hour late," said another politician.

Bobby didn't bother to look up, but he was beginning to burn.

"Maybe he won't show up at all," said a third politician. Bobby spoke.

"There are some envelopes over here!" he snapped at the big politicians. "You want to address them? Fine! Otherwise, you can wait outside! Everybody in this office has a job to do!"

The politicians looked at young Bobby, startled. Then they looked at each other.

"Might as well," said one of them, picking up a batch of the envelopes.

Every one of them grinned and took his own batch of envelopes. The job was soon done.

It may have seemed rude to some; for Bobby every precious moment counted.

"How about those tea parties?" he asked his mother, early in the campaign.

"We're arranging them," said Rose Kennedy.

The first of the famous tea parties was held in the Worcester Sheraton Hotel. All the Kennedy girls, except Kathleen and Rosemary, were there. Pat, who had been working with the NBC Kate Smith Show, gave up her job to work for her brother's election. Eunice gave up her work with prison juveniles to devote herself to the campaign. Jean took a leave from her public-relations job with Father James Keller's Christophers to do her share toward the election of her brother. Kathleen had been killed in a plane crash in France in 1948. Rosemary was at a special school. The others were out in full force.

They wore skirts embroidered with "Vote for Jack Kennedy." They rang doorbells in house-to-house campaigns. They spoke at large mass rallies, and they spoke to small rallies. They spoke in the shopping centers, in the housing developments, in the small stores, wherever they could get the ears of the electorate. And they were effective. The Republicans began to worry.

"Wherever you go, there's a Kennedy. Wherever you look, there's a Kennedy. Wherever you listen, it's a Kennedy doing the talking."

"Did you ever see anyone enjoy a campaign as much as that Rose Kennedy?"

"This is what I call campaigning," answered the mother of the candidate, and her audiences applauded her loudly.

"Do you know that my father, Honey Fitz you called him,

169

never let me talk politics," she said, and her hearers were in on the more intimate details of the family life of the Fitzgeralds and the Kennedys, and they loved it.

"My father used to say that one politician in a family is enough," she said, and her listeners laughed with her. She had won them over, and the votes piled up for her son, Jack Kennedy.

"Eisenhower is going to sweep Massachusetts," all the political pollsters agreed.

Ordinarily, this should have meant a complete sweep for the Republican party in the state, the election of Henry Cabot Lodge and the defeat of Jack Kennedy. But here the pollsters were not so certain.

With election day at hand, they shook their heads and said, "You can't measure anything, the way the Kennedys conducted their campaign. They've been unorthodox, pulled every kind of new political gimmick. We don't know which way this race for the Senate will go."

But the people who went to the polls knew.

Dwight Eisenhower, that most popular of generals, carried Massachusetts, as was predicted. He was the first Republican to win the Bay State for his party since the election of Calvin Coolidge. He carried the whole country. He was elected by a national landslide. Henry Cabot Lodge did not do as well.

Eisenhower took all of Massachusetts' electoral votes by a substantial plurality of 208,800 votes, enough under any normal situation to have elected his senate-candidate with him; but the great campaign, led by young Bobby Kennedy, aided and abetted by "those Kennedy girls," paid off. When the votes of Massachusetts were finally totaled, it was Jack Kennedy the winner by 70,000 tallies. Not only had the young campaigner wiped out the 210,000 plurality won by Eisenhower, but he had taken 280,000 ballots away from the Republican side of the ticket.

"Those darn tea parties," said Henry Cabot Lodge.

"Those blessed tea parties," said Jack Kennedy.

Grandpa Honey Fitz, who died in 1950, could no longer dance a jig on the table, nor could he sing his "Sweet Adeline," but his grandson was carrying on in his tradition, his star in the ascendency, with the ultimate political victory yet to come.

At the age of thirty-six, John Fitzgerald Kennedy took his seat in that august body, the Senate of the United States of

America, junior Senator from the State of Massachusetts. It was a great moment in the history of all the Kennedys. It was a great moment in the life of a young man determined and destined to bring his country to glory.

Back in the capital city, after the tough election campaign, Jack Kennedy took to the two most important tasks in his career: the pursuit of his political obligations and the pursuit of Jacqueline Bouvier. His approach, in both areas, was direct, forthwright, and imbued with that Kennedy will to win.

"You'll have to wait till the Senators get on first," said the attendant as the newly elected Senator from Massachusetts began to move into the elevator cab.

Jack Kennedy smiled.

He just didn't look old enough or gray enough to be a United States Senator.

"My page boy looks more like the picture of a senator than I do," he said, but his voice was loud and clear in the Senate Chambers, and quickly he won his spurs in the upper house of the Congress of our country.

He was a little slower in his campaign to win the hand of Jacqueline Bouvier.

"The greatest thing that happened to me this year," said the young man who had upset all political predictions and beaten Henry Cabot Lodge in the race for one of the most honored political posts in the United States, "the greatest thing that happened to me was meeting Jackie Bouvier."

He phoned her, and he spoke as if it were only hours since he had last said good night.

"Dinner?" he asked, delighted to hear her voice again.

"I'm on my way right now," he said.

The long separation that the battle for the seat in the Senate had created was a thing of the past. It was the theater again and the movies and the long walks and the art galleries. Then Jack Kennedy asked her to marry him.

The wedding of Jacqueline Bouvier, the talented and beautiful young lady from Long Island's Southampton, and John Fitzgerald Kennedy, the handsome and brilliant young Senator from Massachusetts, took place on the twelfth of September, 1953, in the little brownstone gothic St. Mary's Church in Newport, Rhode Island.

There were six hundred guests inside the small church. There were thousands of townspeople and people from the surrounding area who had invited themselves to witness the marriage of the popular young Senator, and they lined the street outside. Senator Leverett Saltonstall, an old friend of the Kennedys, came to the wedding. So did Senator George Smathers of Florida and Speaker of the House of Representatives, Joseph W. Martin, Jr. The church was jammed with celebrities.

Mr. and Mrs. Joseph P. Kennedy, of course, were there. And Bobby Kennedy, with his lovely wife, Ethel Skakel, was there. And Eunice and her husband of only three months, Robert Sargent Shriver, Jr.; and Pat, who was soon to marry the actor Peter Lawford, and Teddy and Jean. Robert Kennedy, of course, was Jack's best man.

The bridal music from Richard Wagner's *Lohengrin* ushered the bride and the groom into the church. Archbishop Richard J. Cushing celebrated the wedding Mass, and as they knelt before the altar in a forty-minute ceremony, he read them a special message cabled from Pope Pius XII.

"The Holy Father on the occasion of this marriage cordially imparts to the Honorable John Fitzgerald Kennedy and Mrs. Kennedy his paternal apostolic blessing in the pledging enduring Christian happiness in married life."

It was indeed an excited and happy bride and groom who left the church to the strains of Mendelssohn's "Wedding March," to the buzz and bustle of the busy and eager press and its photographers, and to the cheers of the thousands of well-wishers who had lined the streets, waiting for them.

Five hundred cars took the wedding guests to the Hammersmith Farm for the reception. Then Jack Kennedy and his wife Jackie quietly took their leave of friends and families, and the next weeks were given to a most happy honeymoon in the warm sunshine of Acapulco, that Edenish garden on the Pacific coast of old Mexico.

After living for a while in Virginia, they set up house in Georgetown, a suburb of Washington.

"It takes Jack just a few minutes to get home," said Jackie. "That's why I like living here."

It was quiet. It was peaceful. It was almost like living in the country.

Jackie took a course in American history. She became a student of the Congressional Record. She translated documents from the French, from the Spanish, to facilitate Jack's work. And Jack took to painting in whatever leisure he had.

173

There was no doubt in Washington that Jack Kennedy had married a woman who was going to be a big asset to him, whatever his political future, whatever his political ambitions.

There was one shadow, however, that cut into the brightness of this happy young marriage. Jack's old injury, the one he had incurred in the Harvard scrimmage, the one that had been aggravated by the explosion on the PT-109, began to act up again. Again, it was the old pain, only this time it was worse. Again, there were the strictures on his physical movement, only this time worse. He didn't want Jackie worried. He tried to conceal his pain. He couldn't. "You'll just have to see a doctor," said Jackie.

He saw a doctor. He saw many doctors. They disagreed in their diagnoses. He began to use crutches, just to get about.

"You can't let this go," insisted Jackie.

He saw another doctor.

"I'd recommend an operation for spinal fusion," said the physician, "except that it's a most difficult, a most delicate operation, and there is nothing guaranteed."

"Just how do you mean that?" asked Jack, his pain now almost insufferable.

"The operation might very well be a success," said the doctor, "yet the patient might die under the ether."

"You don't sound optimistic," said Jack.

"I'll give you the facts, Senator," said the doctor.

Jack talked it over with Jackie.

"This thing is getting worse all the time," he said.

He looked at his crutches.

"I'd rather die than use these the rest of my life."

"You'll not die," said Jackie, controlling her tears.

"I'll not die," said Jack.

He entered the Manhattan Hospital for Special Surgery. Jackie Kennedy was at his side. She remained at his side as long as they permitted her to stay. The operation was performed. It was a delicate operation, and Jackie waited for him to come out of the anesthetic, waited for him to open his eyes.

He was woefully weak. He tried to smile, but he couldn't. The doctors had left the wound in his back open, to drain; it drained for weeks; he was not recovering as well as had been hoped.

"Time, Mrs. Kennedy," the doctor said. "It takes time."

The clock moved slowly; the days and the weeks moved slowly. Jack lay in a darkened room, the only visitors allowed him his wife and his immediate family. There were blood transfusions. There were more blood transfusions.

"Is my husband going to get well?" asked Jackie.

"I think he'll want a priest," said the doctor.

Pale and worn by the ordeal, too distressed to weep, Jackie called a priest. The priest came, and Jack was given the last rites.

"He'll pull through," said Joe Sr., hiding the tears in his eyes.

Rose Kennedy nodded and prayed. Jackie Kennedy prayed. That was all they could do.

"There is a definite turn for the better," said the doctor. "I don't want to give you too much hope," he added quickly, stilling the sudden joy in the hearts of his family, "but for the first time, I think, he had made a definite step toward recovery."

The Kennedys were humble in the face of what seemed to them a miracle, and they prayed, and they were patient, as slowly, painfully slowly, Jack Kennedy came back into the world of the living.

He had entered the hospital on the twenty-first of October. The calendar indicated but a few days left to Christmas.

"I'd like to spend the holidays with my family," he said to the doctor.

"You've got a big family," said the doctor, misunderstanding the request. "I don't think we have the room for them."

Jack smiled.

"They'll all be down in Palm Beach," he explained.

"Oh!" said the doctor. "I don't know. It might be a good idea."

There was a staff consultation, a general agreement, and Jack, warmly dressed, was placed on a stretcher, motored quickly to the airport, and flown down to Florida to be with his family once again.

Christmas was a happy time for Jack, even if he couldn't get about very much, but he was far from well. The pains persisted; the rate of his recovery had slowed down, had stopped.

"I'm afraid, Mr. Senator," said the doctor, "we'll have to operate again."

Again Jack consulted with his wife Jackie. Again they came to the same conclusion.

"I presume," Jack said to the doctor, "this operation will be no less delicate, no less dangerous, than the first."

"Just as delicate. Just as dangerous," said the doctor, "but

175

it is necessary if complete recovery is what you want."

"It's what I want," said Jack.

"I want you to be well," said Jackie.

By the middle of February, Jack Kennedy was back in the hospital, back on the operating table.

"I'd like to see the priest before they operate on me," Jack had said.

Again, Jackie summoned the priest. Again, the priest gave Jack the last rites.

"Better get some rest," said Jack to his wife before they rolled him out of his room for the delicate surgery. "You look very tired."

But Jackie waited. She waited till he came out of the anesthesia. She waited till he got well.

"You're smiling again," she said to him.

"I think this time I'm going to be all right," said Jack.

He was.

This time there were no complications, no long wait in the darkness, no prolonged period of blood transfusions. Before the end of the month, Jack Kennedy was able to walk without the aid of crutches, and he was on his way to Florida once more for the long, long rest that the doctors had ordered.

But the Kennedys never rest. As soon as he could sit up, as soon as he could read a book again, as soon as he could put a pencil to paper, Jack Kennedy was working again.

"John Quincy Adams was a man of great courage," he said to Jackie, looking up from the book he was reading.

Jackie nodded. The man with the greatest courage, and she was most ready to declare it, was her husband.

"I like this Daniel Webster," said Jack. "There was another man of courage, a man of great courage."

The word "courage" came more and more into his thoughts, repeated itself. An idea began to percolate in that quick, alert, ever-busy mind of the young Senator.

"I think I'd like to do a book on these men, these men of courage," he said. "People forget them and what they have meant to the spirit and the temper of our country. I think they need to be reminded of our great men of courage."

"I think," said Jackie, "that you need to be reminded of the doctor's orders. Rest. Do you remember?"

"Of course I remember," said Jack, but his mind was already on his project. "There are some books you can get me, Jackie."

He smiled.

"You will get them for me, won't you?" he asked.

"For a man of courage?" asked Jackie. "How can I refuse?"

The books began to arrive: envelopes with books neatly packed in them, cartons of books neatly stacked, crates of books.

"Where am I going to put them all?" pleaded Jackie.

"Where I can reach them," said Jack.

"Or where I can reach them for you," said Jackie. "Aren't you going at it too hard? Are you really well enough?" she asked.

He wasn't, but the Kennedys never spare themselves, and Jack began to write.

At first it was slow, painfully slow. He tired quickly, much too quickly, and though he would not tell Jackie, he began to think that he had undertaken too big a task for his physical condition. It was his physical condition that disturbed him most and that sometimes sent his normally high spirits into a tailspin. It was in one of these low periods that Jack opened a letter addressed to him by a little old lady of ninety years.

"I've been bedridden for a much longer time than you've been kept to your bed," she wrote from her little Cape Cod village.

She scolded, like the little old grandmother she was, but she was also full of humor and full of hope.

"Never voted for a Democrat in my life, Mr. Kennedy," she wrote, "but I want to vote for at least one before I die— might stand me in good stead up above. So I want you to be up and running in 1958. Don't waste away feeling sorry for yourself, young man. Keep busy. Do all the things you've never had time to do."

It was the greatest dose of tonic Jack Kennedy had ever taken.

"Ninety years old and telling me to keep busy! What do you think of that, Jackie?"

"She must be a Kennedy somewhere along the line," said Jackie, and Jack smiled and got down to work on the book in earnest.

He wrote of John Quincy Adams who, abused and forced to resign from his seat in the Senate because of his forceful stand on the British action against American shipping and sailors on the high seas, fought his battles through, was vindicated, won the plaudits of his countrymen, and was, in his time, elected President of the United States.

He wrote of Daniel Webster who sacrificed his career in

his courageous effort to stop the Civil War; of Edmund G. Ross who cast the deciding vote in the great impeachment hearings on President Andrew Johnson, an act of great courage; of George W. Norris, Protestant and Republican, who stumped for Catholic and Democrat Al Smith, both men of greatest courage; and about others, men of honesty, brave men who courageously and unstintingly waged their wars of conscience and conviction against all.

He titled his book *Profiles in Courage,* and Harper and Brothers, which had turned down *Why England Slept,* took the book quickly. It paid off quickly, and the one-time best-selling author was on the best-seller lists again. This time, there was additional honor. The Pulitzer Prize for the best biography of the year, a coveted prize indeed for all members of the writing profession, was awarded to the Senator from Massachusetts, John Fitzgerald Kennedy.

"Now you're a name in the field of letters," said Jackie, beaming with pride.

And Jack, of course, was pleased, pleased with the prize, more pleased with his contribution to the memory of the men he prized most, those men of conviction and without fear.

He was pleased, too, with his physical condition.

"I think it's time I got back to my job," he said.

"You've been on the job all the time," said Jackie, opening a fresh bottle of milk.

Jack still considered milk an important part of his diet. He always would.

"I mean Washington," he said. "I'd like to get back to my desk in the Senate."

"It seems to me," said Jackie, moving the end table and the milk closer to her husband, "you never left Washington."

And except for the geography of the situation, Jackie Kennedy was completely correct.

Jack's first floor bedroom had long since been converted into an office. On one side of his bed was a multiple phone through which he had kept his contact with Washington constant. On the other side of his bed was a voice-recording machine into which he had dictated letters, among them almost 15,000 replies to inquiries that had flowed into his Washington offices. Almost the moment they had arrived in Palm Beach, the convalescing Senator had called for all information on the action in Congress, particularly, of course, on the action in the Senate. Jack Kennedy wanted to be kept informed on all developments, late and early, both in the domestic and the foreign areas on which he must act, on which he might act at some future date. The Senator from Massachusetts had a responsibility to his constituents back home, to his country, and he meant to discharge it to the very best of his abilities. He meant to be the best Senator he could be!

Nor did Jack Kennedy's political thrust stop with the Senate. He had much time to think, during his long bouts at the hospital, his long periods of enforced rest. His mind had begun to turn to other possibilities in the political life of these United States, but it was still too early for him to talk of them.

First things first, he thought, and before the end of May he returned to active duty on the floor of the United States Senate.

"Let there be no talk about my battles with the hospital," he declared. "I am completely recovered. I am completely well."

He shook hands all around, and his colleagues in the Senate were loud and long, applauding his return. It was like coming back to home base after the sinking of the PT-109.

Lyndon Johnson of Texas, Democratic leader in the Senate, made the first welcoming speech to the young man who had returned from near death once again.

William Knowland, Republican leader of the Senate, added his own sincere words of welcome to the returning Senator from Massachusetts.

The welcome was unanimous, but in no time at all, Jack Kennedy was in there swinging, battling against the policies of the Republican administration, battling for his own point of view and the views of his party.

"The Republicans guessed wrong on Russia's military strength," he charged, his voice strong and firm again.

"The Democratic party will have to develop an effective and positive program if it hopes to make any progress in the 1956 elections," he cautioned his own party colleagues.

He was right in the middle of things, big things. He meant to be heard, and he was heard, and there was considerable evidence, suddenly, that Jack Kennedy of Massachusetts was moving to the top, to the very top, in the life and the politics of his country.

24

There was no doubt as to the naming of the Democratic candidate for the presidency at the 1956 Democratic Convention in Chicago. Adlai Stevenson, beaten by Dwight Eisenhower in the 1952 elections, was scheduled to attempt a reversal in the decision at the polls in the coming November. Jack Kennedy put his name into nomination in the jammed and excited convention hall, made the nominating address. It was Adlai Stevenson by acclamation!

Estes Kefauver, who had become a national figure through his prominent role in Senate investigations, had been Stevenson's only possible rival for the presidential nomination. It seemed only a matter of course that he would be nominated his party's vice-presidential candidate. It didn't come off that easily.

Quietly at first, as if from nowhere, the name of the young Senator from Massachusetts had begun to appear in the press. He was energetic; he was forthright; he knew the issues closest to the hearts and the minds of the people, and he was candid and direct in his attack on those issues. Slowly but persistently, Jack Kennedy became a name with which to reckon. The public was aware of him. It wanted to know more about him. It knew, almost instinctively, that here was a man with destiny at his shoulder.

"He makes sense."

"I like what he says."

Jack was reserved when they spoke of the vice-presidency.

"I think we can do it," said Bobby enthusiastically. "Let's give it a try."

"Let's not go at it too fast," cautioned Jack.

"Now is the time!" insisted Bobby. "And this is the place!"

Jack Kennedy's name was placed in nomination in the big convention hall. His hotel suite was all at once the milling, spilling, hustling, bustling center of an all-out and at-'em election campaign. The Democratic Convention in Chicago was suddenly fired.

As always in an election battle, along with Bobby Kennedy at the helm, there were sisters Eunice and Jean and

Pat, and brother Teddy; and Ted Sorensen was there. Sorensen had been hired by Jack in 1953. A capable lawyer, writer, and research man whose father was the Attorney General of Nebraska, Ted became an integral part of the Kennedy "brain trust." John Bailey, the National Chairman of the Democratic party, and brother-in-law Sargent Shriver were also there.

"It's like old times at the Cape," said Pat.

"All for one and one for all," said Jean.

Someone pushed in through the crowd in the hotel suite. "Georgia has caucused. They're voting for Jack Kennedy!"

A loud roar of approval greeted the electrifying news, but the calmer voice of Jack Kennedy broke through it.

"Not Georgia? Are you sure it's Georgia?"

Georgia was South. Georgia was scarcely inclined to vote a Catholic into nomination.

"Georgia!" repeated the bearer of good tidings. "I've just come from their meeting! They gave me their word on it!"

It was hard to believe, but it was true, and the clamor rose again in the headquarters of the young Senator from Massachusetts. They smelled victory, and their voices rose to it.

"What do you say now?" shouted Sargent Shriver.

"You're in!" yelled Bob Kennedy.

"Let's say for now that I'm a candidate for the nomination," said Jack Kennedy soberly. "This thing can still go anywhere and to anyone."

Jack was reserved, but he couldn't quiet the enthusiasm of his great campaigners. No one in his hotel suite slept that night. There was too much that had to be done, too much to do.

Albert Gore was nominated for the second place on his party's ticket. Hubert Humphrey of Minnesota was nominated. Estes Kefauver and Robert Wagner had already been placed in nomination. It was a free-for-all, and Jack Kennedy was right. There was no telling which way the convention was going to wind up.

He stayed behind in his suite, feverishly working at his papers, but his people kept him constantly informed of the struggle on the floor of the convention hall.

"They're beginning to vote!" shouted Eunice, coming into the room in a rush, drinking a quick glass of milk, and returning as quickly to the scene of the balloting.

"Four hundred eighty-three and one-half votes for Kefauver!" shouted Ted Sorensen, returning with the tally of the first count. "Three hundred and four for Kennedy! We'll get them on the next ballot!"

Six hundred and eighty-six votes would decide the victor in the race. The Kennedy forces had their work cut out for them. They cornered the Humphrey supporters. They moved in among the Gore voters. They turned to the men and women who had cast their ballots for Wagner. These were the votes that would make the difference, and they went out after them.

"They're beginning the second go-around!" announced Pat.

The unexpected strength of Jack Kennedy had startled the entire convention. The voting was loud. The voting was noisy.

"Texas . . . 56 votes for the Senator from Massachusetts, Jack Kennedy!"

Pandemonium broke loose on the floor of the gigantic convention hall.

Now Kennedy, now Kefauver, added to his total; now Kennedy, now Kefauver, neared the magic number: 686.

Again it was Ted Sorensen who came back to the hotel suite, Jack Kennedy's campaign headquarters, with the news of the tally.

"Jack Kennedy," he shouted, "618 votes! Kefauver, 551½! One more time and we have it!"

Jack was still. That one more time might not be his. Conventions have been known to be fickle, and young Kennedy knew it.

"We've got to keep moving!" declared Bob Kennedy. "We've got to move!"

There was no time to be wasted, no time to be lost. The third tally was already under way.

"Kentucky . . . 30 votes for John Kennedy."

"New York . . . 98 votes for the Senator from Massachusetts!"

"That's it!" shouted Sargent Shriver. "You're in!"

Jack started to put on his coat.

Ohio was next.

"Ohio coasts 51½ votes for Estes Kefauver, 5½ for Kennedy!"

Jack took off his coat.

Tennessee called for the floor.

"The chairman recognizes the delegate from the State of Tennessee.

"Mr. Chairman, Tennessee requests the opportunity for

182

its candidate, Albert Gore, to make a brief announcement."

And Senator Gore electrified the convention.

"With thanks to this great, free Democratic Convention, I request that my name be withdrawn in favor of my colleague, Senator Estes Kefauver!"

"That's it!" said Jack.

Oklahoma went over to Kefauver; Hubert Humphrey's Minnesota went over to Kefauver.

The bandwagon was rolling.

Missouri went over to Kefauver.

Jack Kennedy and his party raced down the back steps, got into the convention hall through a back door, and Jack managed to find a seat on the platform.

"Mr. Chairman."

Senator Sam Rayburn, chairman of the convention, recognized him.

"Senator Kennedy."

Jack moved to the microphones.

A deafening roar greeted him.

He smiled faintly, waved to his friends yelling themselves hoarse in the crowd.

"Gentlemen," he began.

He spoke without notes. He spoke briefly and to the point, as always.

This was his first defeat, but he knew how to meet it.

"Mr. Chairman," he said, "I move that we suspend the rules and make the nomination of Senator Estes Kefauver by acclamation."

A mighty roar of approval shook the convention hall to its foundations, and the approval was for Jack Kennedy's resolution and the approval was for Jack Kennedy the man. All at once, that historic day in Chicago, the young Senator from Massachusetts had become a Democratic statesman and a man for the nation to applaud and admire.

"No, I don't like losing," Jack said later, but there were few, very few, who thought the young Senator had lost at all. The place on the ballot was not his in 1956, but the prestige he had won for himself was immeasurable.

In 1958, he campaigned again for his Senatorial seat from Massachusetts, and the Bay State showed the nation what it thought of the young Jack Kennedy. It piled up the tremendous majority of almost 875,000 votes for its young statesman, the greatest majority ever recorded in a Massachusetts election. It catapulted him into a leading position in his party. It made him a certainty in the battle for the Democratic nomination for president in 1960.

"He's the man all right!"

"He's the man to beat Ike or anyone else the Republicans put up against him!"

The man in the street, the press, radio, television—all were eager for copy on the young Kennedy. They couldn't get enough.

"THE SPOTLIGHT IS ON KENNEDY."

"JACK KENNEDY FACES THE ISSUES."

"KENNEDY FRONT RUNNER."

Even before his candidacy was announced, the public had begun to divide itself, pro and con Jack Kennedy.

Hubert Humphrey announced himself a candidate for the Democratic nomination for the presidency. Jack Kennedy beat him handily in the state primaries, where Humphrey's strength was assumed to be greatest.

Estes Kefauver announced his candidacy, but he gave ground to the growing surge of votes for the Senator from Massachusetts.

In West Virginia and Wisconsin, where religious bias against Jack Kennedy was expected to count heavily against him, the young candidate swept both states with startling majorities.

There was only one man who stood between Kennedy and his party's nomination. That man was Adlai Stevenson. Much of the heart of the party was with the man who had twice carried the banner for the Democrats in the national campaign; but Stevenson had lost twice, and his opponent had swept into power with landslide majorities.

"It has to be Kennedy!"

"Kennedy is the man!"

"It's Kennedy for President!"

"Kennedy!"

On the very first ballot in the great convention hall, the Democrats went wild with jubilation.

"Kennedy!"

"Kennedy!"

"Kennedy!"

There was a brief surge of Stevenson strength. But it was Kennedy by acclamation! A great acclamation!

Nomination, however, is not election, and Jack Kennedy faced the toughest fight of his political career, the toughest battle in history for the presidency of the United States.

Bobby Kennedy, of course, was once more at the helm,

directing the national campaign to elect his brother, and he gave it all his youthful energy, all his will to win. Larry O'Brien and Ted Reardon were with the team, and Ted Sorensen, Torb Macdonald, Les Billings, Rip Horton—all the old friends of the Harvard days and a host of new ones. Ted Kennedy dropped all his activities to take charge of the Middle West. Eunice and Pat and Jean gave up all their private interests for the time being. And Rose Kennedy, now sixty-nine years old, once again took to the political platforms to bring the vote in for her son.

"I'll go wherever they want me to go. I'll speak wherever they want me to speak. I'm all out for Jack!"

So was everyone in the camp of Jack Kennedy, but Rose Kennedy brought it that extra unorthodox touch.

She spoke of her seventeen grandchildren more than she did of the political issues, but her audiences loved her. More important to her, they loved Jack, and they told her so.

The Kennedys were past masters at the art of unorthodox campaign. Though they were as good as any at the tried and true methods of electioneering, it was at the unorthodox that they were best.

It was the completely unorthodox debates between Republican candidate Richard Nixon and the Democrats' Jack Kennedy, produced on television and viewed by millions and millions of voters, that may have been the deciding factor in the closest American presidential election in history. Nixon, with the personal prestige of Dwight Eisenhower behind him, lost ground in those debates. This was the general consensus. But how much ground?

The biggest election question was not to be answered till all the votes were in: Could a young Kennedy, could a Catholic, overcome the popularity of the man backed by Eisenhower, as well as the prejudice that had swamped the only other Catholic ever to run for the presidency, Alfred E. Smith of the brown derby?

The pre-election campaign raged mercilessly on all issues, in all areas, with no quarter asked and no quarter given. Sixteen hours a day, eighteen hours a day, and seven days in the week, from sunup to sundown, Nixon and his cohorts, Kennedy and his cohorts, ranged the length and breadth of our country. By car, by train, by plane, the rival candidates spared nothing at all to reach the eyes and the ears of the American electorate.

"It's going to be close," said the man on the street.

"It's going to be mighty close," said his neighbor.

"It looks as though it will go right down to the wire, and you can make your choice. I can't predict who is going to win the election," said the political forecasters.

For once they were right.

This was the hottest race, the closest race, the American people had ever witnessed.

25

Some seventy million Americans went to the polls on November 7, 1960, farmers, mill-workers, teachers, lawyers, housewives, men and women of every rank and title, to cast the ballot so sacred to every citizen of the United States. From Maine to California, from Louisiana to Minnesota, from up north in the new state of Alaska and out over the Pacific to the new state of Hawaii, the main job of the day was to pull that lever, write in that name, to elect the next president of our country, the most honored, the most responsible job an American can ever dream of attaining. Sometimes predictions as to the outcome of the election can be made with fair accuracy. Sometimes, though less often, the election is a foregone conclusion before the balloting begins. This year of 1960, nobody knew for sure; nobody could even guess.

"It's a toss-up."

"Who knows?"

"Maybe Kennedy."

"Maybe Nixon."

This is all anyone could say. The country voted and the country settled itself before its radios and television sets to listen to the reports as they came from their home districts, their home towns, from neighboring states, from cities and states thousands of miles away, eagerly, hopefully, impatiently.

And the Kennedys were listening, too, and watching, and counting. Robert Kennedy's house in Hyannisport, Massachusetts, had become headquarters for the returns, and long hours before the voting was all done, the TV equipment had been set, extra telephones, electronic equipment, and an army of technicians along with it, had been installed, ready for use. Campaign workers and family mingled in quiet, strained anticipation. Messengers appeared out of nowhere, were suddenly gone again, and new messengers took their places.

"Testing. Testing."

"The state tabulators are right here."

"I've the direct line all set."

"Ready now?"

The whole country was ready. The first districts were beginning to send in their tallies.

It was only a scattering of votes, but the huge and complicated electronic calculators began their predictions immediately.

"According to these very early figures," announced the solemn gentleman, speaking into the microphones of one of the larger TV networks in the country, "our electronic computer predicts the next President of the United States will be Richard Nixon. Right now, the voting, though only a minute percentage of the total vote cast, indicates a Nixon sweep by thirty-two to one!"

"They ought to get that machine out of here!" scowled Bobby Kennedy.

He was tired. They were all tired. The campaign had taken them into forty-eight states, and in some of the states they had made more than one great bid for the votes of their citizens. They were campaign-weary, and their nerves were on edge.

"Maybe they ought to get somebody who knows how to operate it!" said Robert.

Then he grinned.

"It'll take a lot more counting before we know anything about this election," he said. "And then we'll know that we've won!"

It took a lot of counting; and more than that. More than 71,000,000 people sat in front of their TV sets well into the early hours of the morning, and still the country was without a definitely elected president. Some spent the night without sleep and sat with their morning coffee in their laps, waiting for that final victory signal; and they did not get it. It was indeed a night and a morning for the country to remember.

At 6:54, Eastern Standard Time, the evening of the election, the John Daly news show announced that Univac predicted the election of Nixon, with the odds favoring him by ten to one.

But only three-tenths of one per cent of the electorate had been counted.

By 8:22 of the same evening, NBC announced, "The odds in favor of Kennedy's election are six to one."

"Now that's a nice robot," said Bobby Kennedy.

The seesaw had begun. Now Kennedy in the lead, now Nixon.

The Atlantic states were reporting. Connecticut was the first.

188

Abe Ribicoff promised, "We'll take the state by 100,000."

He missed by a mere 10,000. Connecticut came in for John Kennedy.

A spontaneous burst of applause; Connecticut had delivered its eight electoral votes.

The next president of the United States would need to garner 261 of the 520 votes to be cast at the next meeting of the Electoral College. Connecticut and its eight were very welcome, but where do we go from here?

"Massachusetts . . . 16 votes . . . Kennedy!"

"Rhode Island . . . 4 votes . . . Kennedy!"

"Maine . . . 5 votes . . . Nixon!"

"New Hampshire . . . 4 votes . . . Nixon!"

No real surprises. Nothing really unexpected.

"Wait till the big states begin to come in," said Jack Kennedy to his brother.

The big states were New York, 45 votes, Pennsylvania, 32 votes, Illinois, 27 votes, Texas, 24 votes.

It was going to be a long night, a long wait, and then some more of the same.

Then, of a sudden, there appeared to be a marked trend in the returns. New Jersey came in for Kennedy. Jack had hoped for it, but it came as something of a surprise.

"You really didn't expect it?" said Bobby.

"I've got it," said Jack.

He took Pennsylvania. He took New York. Texas came to Kennedy, and Maryland. John F. Kennedy had amassed 260 electoral votes. He needed a mere nine more, and he was the next President of the United States. Bob Kennedy's house was alive with the noise and the commotion of congratulations.

"Not yet," said Jack. "The vote is not all in."

He was right.

Florida went to Nixon. Iowa went to Nixon. Ohio, which had seemed to go Kennedy, suddenly veered into the Nixon column. The new states, Alaska and Hawaii, went to Nixon.

Where is Illinois? Where is Minnesota? California was completely undecided.

It was past three in the morning. The count had simmered down.

"Close," said Bobby, his eyes fixed on the teletype machine. "But we'll win! We'll win!"

Jack was too tired to answer. He simply grinned.

"Why don't you go to bed?" said Bobby. "I'll wake you up if there's any news."

The teletype began to chatter. The TV blared full blast.

"We expect a statement by Vice-President Nixon at any moment."

Bobby came alive in his chair. "Jack, here it is now; here we go!"

Jack Kennedy did not stir.

The TV cameras turned on the enormous crowd at the Nixon headquarters. Nobody was leaving anywhere that night, not before the news of the election was definite.

"This is it," whispered Bobby.

Jack said nothing.

The noise of the Nixon party was loud and demanding. There was no note of defeat among them.

"The Vice-President should be coming down this aisle momentarily," announced the TV speaker. "And here he is!"

The applause, the shouting of his supporters, began before he actually appeared. It was deafening as he walked into the room with his wife Pat.

Bobby moved to cut down the volume, but he stopped.

"What have they got to cheer about?" he asked himself angrily.

Jack's eyes were glued on the screen and on the face of the man he had battled through every state in the Union.

"He looks as tired as I feel," he said.

Richard Nixon was tired, but he was not defeated. At least, he was not ready to concede his defeat.

He waved his hands to the crowd, let it cheer its candidate, then asked for silence.

"Here it comes," said one of Kennedy's campaigners.

The whole roomful was watching the TV set now. This was the big moment, the biggest, the moment for Nixon to congratulate the winner of the great election. It did not come.

If he was the loser, Richard Nixon did not know it.

"My wife and I," he announced simply, "are retiring for the night."

The TV set carried a roar of cheering.

The crowd at the Bob Kennedy house did not cheer.

"What's he waiting for?"

"He's licked and he doesn't know it!"

"Concede! Concede!" they shouted at the TV screen angrily.

"Why should he?"

It was Jack Kennedy speaking.

"Take it easy, men. There's still some counting to be done."

The Kennedy cohorts quieted, went back to their jobs of computing and calculating and computing some more.

"Do you want to make a statement?" Pierre Salinger, Jack Kennedy's press secretary, asked of him. "These people have been working and waiting all night. Something about a victory might pick them up a bit."

Jack thought a moment. His colleagues had certainly put in a lot of work, this night and the months of nights before. It would be warming to him and to them, both, to be able to say, "We've won!"

He shook his head.

"Not now," he said. "It'll have to wait."

Protocol demanded that the victor keep the silence till the loser conceded. If nothing more, it was the polite gesture to a valiant antagonist.

"I guess I'll go to bed, too," he grinned wearily.

He was confident that he had won the election. Still, it was not a certainty, even at that late hour.

"Good night," he waved to his no less weary election crew. "Or rather, good morning."

He walked across the lawn of his brother Bobby's house, climbed the stairs to his own bedroom, and gently opened the door.

Jacqueline was awake.

"I've been dozing," she said. "I can't really fall asleep. Is it all over, Jack?"

She didn't dare ask who had won.

"Illinois is shaky," said Jack. "California isn't all in yet. Better get some rest, Jacqueline."

"You're not sure?"

"I think we have it."

"But you're not singing it?"

"We'll know for certain soon. You're tired, Jackie. Get some sleep."

"You're tired yourself, Mr. President."

"Exhausted," said Jack, reaching for his overcoat. "I'll just take a short walk. Clear my head a bit. Get some sleep, Jackie."

The night was still dark in Hyannisport, but the early sun would soon break through. He drew the collar of his coat tight against the chill of the sharp November air and walked down toward the water.

The way was familiar. How many times had he taken this walk since his childhood? How many times had he run and tumbled across this green lawn with his brothers and sisters? How many times had he swum in these Nantucket Sound waters, sailed in them, raced in them?

191

He recalled his older brother Joe, his rival and his closest friend. Joe was dead now, killed in an heroic mission against the enemy sixteen years ago. In moments of victory, the remembrance of a grievous loss will sometimes demand its place in the celebration. There were other moments of grief for Jack to remember, and moments that were warm and to be treasured for other reasons.

There was Grandpa Fitzgerald and Grandpa Kennedy, two men who had bulled their way through Boston politics. There was his own father, a man of great pride and determination, perhaps the strongest influence in his life. There was his mother, gentle but firm, loving and ambitious for her children. There was Jackie, who was sleeping now at last after the grueling months of tough campaigning, after the long cruel night, counting the ballots, waiting on returns, and counting again, hoping and hoping and never certain of what the day would bring them. And there was three-year-old Caroline, only vaguely aware of the meaning of the excitement and the tension in her household. There was the child to be born in some three weeks.

Jack Kennedy looked up into the sky. The blackness of the night was beginning to give way to the gray of morning.

"Thank you, Lord . . ."

Quietly he spoke the words of the prayer he had learned, as a boy, from his mother.

There was peace in the skies and peace in Hyannisport. But in the world, scarcely a continent was without its trouble spot: Laos in Asia, Berlin in Europe, Cuba in the Western Hemisphere, three major problems. There were others: China, Russia, Algeria, the whole wide stretch of Africa, and more. And at home, there was the growing army of unemployed.

The presidency of the United States, in normal times, is the most strenuous, the most demanding political position in the entire world. In times of stress and peril its duties and obligations are near to superhuman.

This was the position that fell to John Fitzgerald Kennedy the seventh of November in the year 1960. As the world looks to America to lead it in its fight for peace and freedom, so the people of the United States look to its president.

John Kennedy turned slowly from the Nantucket waters and made his way home, the man his country had elected its thirty-fifth president.

★ ★ ★